Romance Authors

For Reference

Not to be taken from this room

**Recent Titles in the
Author Research Series**
Jen Stevens, Series Editor

Fantasy Authors: A Research Guide
Jen Stevens and Dorothea Salo

Science Fiction Authors: A Research Guide
Maura Heaphy

Women's Fiction Writers: A Research Guide
Rebecca Vnuk

Romance Authors:
A Research Guide

Sarah E. Sheehan

Author Research Series
Jen Stevens, Series Editor

AN IMPRINT OF ABC-CLIO, LLC
Santa Barbara, California • Denver, Colorado • Oxford, England

Library of Congress Cataloging-in-Publication Data

Sheehan, Sarah E.
Romance authors : a research guide / Sarah E. Sheehan.
   p. cm. — (Author research series)
   Includes bibliographical references and index.
   ISBN 978-1-59884-386-6 (acid-free paper)   1. Love stories, American—Bio-bibliography—
Dictionaries.   2. Love stories, English—Bio-bibliography—Dictionaries.   I. Title.
   PS374.L6S54   2010
   813'.08509—dc22   2010028714

ISBN: 978-1-59884-386-6

14   13   12   11   10   1   2   3   4   5

This book is also available on the World Wide Web as an eBook.
Visit www.abc-clio.com for details.

Libraries Unlimited
An Imprint of ABC-CLIO, LLC

ABC-CLIO, LLC
130 Cremona Drive, P.O. Box 1911
Santa Barbara, California 93116-1911

This book is printed on acid-free paper ∞

Manufactured in the United States of America

Contents

Introduction

Romance Authors: A Research Guide is intended for romance fans and researchers in search of a starting place in studying a specific author or the genre itself; and librarians assisting patrons in finding new authors or out-of-print titles.

Romance is the Rodney Dangerfield of genres. We just don't get much respect, as either a reader or a writer. Accordingly, finding scholarly, research sources for the romance genre can be difficult. Although the genre is starting to receive some critical treatment from academia more recently, there still isn't much available yet. It is my hope that *Romance Authors: A Research Guide* will be a valuable part of the nascent scholarly research available for romance authors and the romance genre.

What Makes a Romance Novel?

The Romance Writers of America[1] list two criteria:
1. A central love story
2. An emotionally satisfying and optimistic ending

Contrary to the stereotype, romance novels are not written by formula nor are they required to stick to a specific formula. Conventions are followed, including the happy ending, but the way that the couple gets there is always different. There may be dancing at *Almacks* in a Regency, guns blazing in a Western, or a dead body in a Romantic Suspense, but the love story between the hero and the heroine always remain the focus of the story.

Mary Balogh, Stephanie Laurens, Candice Hern, and Jacquie D'Alessandro put this stereotype to the test in the 2008 anthology *It Happened One Night.*

Each story has the same plot, a couple who have known each other for over 10 years that end up stranded for 24 hours at the same inn. Each story is very different with older heroines, broken-hearted lovers reunited, and a married couple who have not seen each other in over 10 years. *It Happened One Night* is a wonderful example of the individual nature of each romance story.

History and Trends

The romance novel has a long history. Shakespeare's comedies are romance stories with the couple happily married at the end. Jane Austen's *Sense and Sensibility* (1811), gave the romance story its structure. However, the modern romance novel era began with the publication of Kathleen E. Woodiwiss's *The Flame and the Flower* in 1972. That publication, which was longer than the Mills & Boon novels that featured the virgin heroine and playboy/doctor/millionaire hero, contained sex and marked a change in the romance stories published for women.

The pejorative term for these first novels was the *bodice ripper,* and the sexy covers feature poses by the hero and heroine that could not be held by any flesh and blood person. They certainly weren't anatomical. The covers of romance novels have alternatively been glorified with cover models like Fabio and vilified due to the overflowing bodices and unnatural bodies of the heroes and heroines. In the 2000s, romance novel covers evolved from the clinch covers to landscapes and the graceful display of women's backs. Historically accurate covers rarely exist and the models reflect current standards of beauty.

Just as with the covers, what's inside the books has changed as well. Gone are the rape stories, the too-stupid-to-live heroines, and the overbearing, alpha males. Today, heroines are just as likely to save the hero as to be saved. The heroes are more sensitive and welcome the intelligence and strength of the heroines.

A trend that has had benefits as well as drawbacks is the publishers reprinting the older books of established authors. Reprints are a wonderful benefit to the romance reader by providing access to an author's backlist of out-of-print titles. But, as stated above, times change and readers' sensibilities change. A reprint of a Linda Howard *Silhouette Intimate Moments* category novel from 1992 is very different from a Linda Howard romantic suspense title published in 2010. Readers may expect one thing and end up buying something different. Moreover, new covers always come with the reprints, making something old seem like something new. Be sure to check the copyright date of all romance novels before purchase. More than once, a reader has purchased a reprinted title of a beloved author only to realize that she already owned it or that it featured characterizations that don't reflect today's sensibilities.

There are several books that have taken on the history of the romance novel. Jayne Ann Krentz wrote a wonderful introduction to the romance genre in 1982 entitled *Dangerous Men and Adventurous Women*. This slim paperback is required reading for the romance researcher and the curious romance fan.

In 2003, Pamela Regis wrote *A Natural History of the Romance Novel* a scholarly study on romance from the 18th century to the modern day.

For an entertaining and irreverent look at the romance novel, consider Sarah Wendell and Candy Tan's, *Beyond Heaving Bosoms: The Smart Bitches Guide to Romance Novels*. Wendell and Tan are the pair behind the *Smart Bitches, Trashy Books* blog, and provide a wonderfully entertaining review of the romance novel.

Organization of Entries

Author entries are arranged alphabetically by the author's most commonly used name which may or may not be the author's original name. This is done because several authors publish under more than one name or use pseudonyms so that readers will not be confused when an author writes in a different subgenre (i.e., Jayne Ann Krentz writes contemporary novels under her real name, historical novels under the pseudonym Amanda Quick, and futuristic stories by the name Jayne Castle).

Each author's work is categorized by the popular subgenres used to identify romance novels. (For a further breakdown of the subgenres see below).

Next, the entry contains a brief biographical sketch of the author. Following that is a list of her works in reverse chronological order, including nonfiction works and any novels that may have been made into films.

The Research Sources section contains encyclopedia articles, interviews with the author conducted online or in print, and any criticism available. Academic research sources such as *Literature Resource Center, MLA Bibliography, and Dissertation Abstracts* among others were consulted to create the list. Web sites, such as *All About Romance,* were included to add depth. In many cases, these Web sites were the only research sources available.

One definite lack within the Research Sources category was that *Romantic Times Book Reviews* magazine, the main industry magazine, is not indexed in any academic source. Due to the lack of access to *Romantic Times,* many interviews with authors were not available for this work.

If an author has a personal Web site and/or blog, it is mentioned in the entry. Some authors do not have a Web site, and in that case I included fan sites if available.

Romance Novel Subgenres

Author entries include a list of romance subgenres, historical, medieval, Regency, western, contemporary, romantic suspense, category, futuristic, and inspirational. Many authors write across the subgenres or incorporate two subgenres together. Nora Roberts publishes romantic suspense novels set in a futuristic setting under the pseudonym J. D. Robb. In turn, Jude Deveraux's classic *A Knight in Shining Armor* begins as a contemporary and uses time travel to transport her heroine to the Middle Ages.

Subgenres may have conventions of style that alert the reader to the type of story available.

A Historical romance novel can take place in any time period in the past, anywhere in the world. The hero or heroine can be nobility and is usually wealthy, but some authors do write about the lives of ordinary people. Within the historical subgenre, the novels are further defined by time period. Popular historical novels range from the pirate stories of the 1970s up to sexier versions of the Regency novel published in the 2000s. Julia Quinn, Johanna Lindsey, and Amanda Quick all write entertaining stories using historical settings.

The three most popular categories of historical novels are the Regency, medieval, and western.

The Regency novel takes place during the Regency period from 1811 to 1837 in England, when George the III was incapable of fulfilling the obligations as king and his son was installed at the Prince Regent. Regency novels generally follow the style of Georgette Heyer. The couple generally is from the *ton,* the aristocracy of the time, and sex before marriage rarely, if ever, happens. The lack of graphic sex is one element the separates the Regency from a historical novel. Mary Balogh's early works and any Candice Hern novel are wonderful examples of the Regency subgenre.

Medieval novels were popular in the 1990s. Medieval romance novels cover the time period from 400 to 1470 and the best include accurate portrayals of historical events of the time period. Any Roberta Gellis novel, as well as Elizabeth Lowell's Untamed series are wonderful examples of medieval romance novels.

The western romance novel was popular in the 1980s and the 1990s, and some authors continue to find audiences with the setting in the 2000s, especially in combination with the inspirational subgenre. The symbolic American cowboy and his hard-working woman are the characteristics of this subgenre. With a rise in historical accuracy in many of the novels, the Native American has become hero material instead of the villain. Johanna Lindsey has written some entertaining westerns with Native American heroes.

Contemporary romance novels were popularized through the Mills & Boon stories in England and the Harlequin category stories in the United States, and now occupy a large part of the romance novel field. Contemporary novels are stories that take place today and feature the modern woman as the heroine. Thus, a contemporary novel written in 1980 is very different from a contemporary novel written in 2010. Society changes and the romance novel changes with society.

In the contemporary novel subgenre, the most popular categories are romantic suspense novels, stories with paranormal elements, the category story, and the inspirational novels.

The romantic suspense novels helped produce heroines who are tough, if not tougher than the heroes. These women survive tough situations, can fire a gun, and save the hero as often as the hero rescues the heroine. While the mystery or action adventure is important in the romantic suspense novel, the love story between the hero and heroine is always the main plot. Romantic suspense novels can be considered the modern-day version of the Gothic novels of the 19th and early 20th centuries. Suzanne Brockmann's *Troubleshooter* novels and Nora Roberts writing as J. D. Robb's *In Death* series are entertaining romantic suspense stories.

Paranormal novels have so far been the hot sellers in the 2000s. Vampires, werewolves, ghosts, and time travel are all variations on the paranormal story. Time travel stories have been a popular plot convention over the history of romance novels, and Jude Deveraux's *Knight in Shining Armor* is a wonderful example. Christina Skye has one of the most interesting ghosts in print in Adrian Draycott, the guardian ghost in the Draycott Abbey series.

The category novel consists of the stories found in the checkout line in the grocery store and the different lines from Harlequin denote the type of story found between the covers. A few examples of a category novel would be the very steamy and sexy Harlequin Blaze stories; Harlequin Intrigue line, with stories that include a mystery plot; and Silhouette Special Edition stories that focus on the heroine's effort to balance her life.

Category novels are short, entertaining reads and are the real culprit of the stereotype of the romance genre. From the nurse/doctor stories of the 1960s to the cowboy/soldier/sheik stories of the 2000s, the category novel has routinely been the black sheep of the publishing world. Except it sells. It sells HUGE. Women (and some men) love the category novel. According to the 2005 Market Research Study produced by the Romance Writers of America, 54.9 percent of all paperback novels sold were romance titles, including category titles, (Romance Writers of America, Market Research Study on Romance Readers brochure 2005). Most of the current best-selling authors who publish in hardback began writing in category, including Jayne Ann Krentz, Linda Howard, and Nora Roberts.

The futuristic story is the romance novel's answer to science fiction. It usually features women who are intelligent and vitally important to the future world, and not just as arm candy. Johanna Lindsey wrote some fun futuristics in the 1980s and Jayne Ann Krentz writes futuristic stories as Jayne Castle.

The inspirational novel is new to the romance genre and unlike the other romance subgenres, inspirational stories have their own publishers. The stories feature heroes and heroines with a strong belief in Christian values. Usually one of main characters has strayed from a belief in God and his or her renewal in faith is as important as the love story. Inspirational stories rarely have premarital sex.

Selection Criteria

The authors selected for this guide represent both American and International romance authors who have published significant titles in the 20th and 21st centuries with select additions of notable historical authors. Authors were selected from several sources, including winners of the Romance Writers of America Lifetime Achievement award, authors who routinely appear on the "Top 100" lists of both *The Romance Reader* and *All About Romance* Web sites, and historical authors listed as influences by today's writers. The initial list generated contained well over 100 names, and narrowing the scope down to 50 was a difficult process. Unfortunately, some classic authors such as Victoria Holt and best-selling authors such as Laura Kinsale and Christina Dodd had to be left off.

While the focus is on romance authors writing today, the history of the genre cannot be ignored. One can draw a rather straight, literary line from Jane Austen to Georgette Heyer to Mary Balogh. A similar line runs from the Brontë sisters to Daphne du Maurier to Linda Howard. The past feeds the present and that is very true in romance novels.

Note

1. "About the Romance Genre." Romance Writers of America. http://www. rwanational.org/cs/the_romance_genre/. Last visited June 2010.

Romance Timeline

Literary Events	World Events
	400–1485—Medieval period
1787–1792—Mary Wollstonecraft publishes *Thoughts on the Education of Daughters* and *A Vindication of the Rights of Woman.*	1714–1830—Georgian period 1775–1783—American Revolution
1811–1817—Jane Austen publishes her works *Sense & Sensibility, Pride and Prejudice, Mansfield Park, Emma, Persuasion, Northanger Abbey.*	1803–1815—Napoleonic Wars 1811–1837—Regency period 1837–1901—Victorian era 1861–1865—American Civil War April 1889—Oklahoma land rush
Brontë sisters publish their works.	
1917—Georgette Heyer publishes her first work, *The Black Moth.*	1914–1918—World War I August 18, 1920—19th Amendment—women get the right to vote.
1936—Margaret Mitchell publishes *Gone with the Wind.*	
1938—Daphne du Maurier publishes *Rebecca.* Alfred Hitchcock directs the academy award winning movie in 1940.	1939–1945—World War II

Literary Events	World Events
1949—Simone de Beauvoir publishes *The Second Sex.*	
1963—Margaret Mead publishes *Sex and Temperament in Three Primitive Societies.*	November 22, 1963—JFK Assassination
1963—Betty Friedan publishes *The Feminine Mystique.*	
1966—Jacqueline Susan publishes *Valley of the Dolls.*	1967—Summer of Love
1971—Mills and Boon is purchased by Harlequin Enterprises.	1971–1973—*Roe v. Wade* is affirmed by the Supreme Court.
1972—Kathleen Woodiwiss publishes *The Flame and the Flower.*	1972—Equal Rights Amendment is approved by Congress.
1980—Bertrice Small publishes *Skye O'Malley.*	
1981—Kathryn Faulk begins *Romantic Times* magazine.	
1981—The Romance Writers of America hold their first conference in Houston, Texas.	
1982—The first annual Romantic Times Booklovers' Convention was held in New York City	
1987—Fabio appears on his first book cover, *Hearts Aflame* by Johanna Lindsey	
1992—Jayne Ann Krentz edits *Dangerous Men and Adventurous Women*	August 2, 1990–February 28, 1991 — First Gulf War
1994—Loretta Chase publishes *Lord of Scoundrels*	
1995—Nora Roberts publishes *The Pride of Jared McKay,* the 1000 novel in the Silhouette Special Edition series	1996—Madeleine Albright becomes the first secretary of state, appointed by President Bill Clinton.

Literary Events	World Events
1997—The All About Romance Listserv begins	
1997—Nora Roberts sues Janet Dailey over plagiarism. The lawsuit is settled out of court	
	September 11, 2001—The World Trade Center and the Pentagon are attacked. United Airlines Flight 93 crashes in Pennsylvania.
	2003—invasion of Iraq
2004—Jennifer Crusie publishes *Bet Me*	
March 2005—The *Smart Bitches, Trashy Books* blog begins	
October 2008—The *At the Back Fence* column at the *All About Romance* website ends	
2009—International Association for the Study of Popular Romance was founded	January 20, 2009—Barack Obama becomes president.

How to Use this Book

The book is meant for fans of the romance genre, as well as librarians, and researchers looking for a place to start the research process. Book club leaders may also find it useful.

Romance Readers

You may browse the author entries, looking for favorites, and for authors of a similar subgenre. The complete back list of each author is especially important for romance readers. Most category titles of established authors can only be found in used bookstores or on eBay. In used bookstores the books are usually shelved by category series, for example, Silhouette Intimate Moments and then series number. This information is rarely available on author's Web sites, and it helps readers with the reprint issue.

Students or Researchers

You may browse the author entries for ideas and for research sources for your projects. As romance is the Rodney Dangerfield of fiction, little serious research was done in the past but that is now beginning to change. Because of the lack of traditional scholarly research, a lot of Web sites were used to identify additional sources, mainly interviews. Some of the most interesting information about the authors and their stories was obtained from these interviews. The *Bibliography of Sources* is a good place to start any research project.

Librarians

Thank you for picking up this book. The list of authors' major works, including the list of category novels will help you answer patrons' questions. In addition, several of the entries have a *You May Like* section to assist you in helping patrons with what to read next.

Book Club Leaders

You may browse through the book to find authors or books for your club. The many *You May Like* sections will help you find similar authors for your readers. Also, the interviews and biographies will be of interest to you. Also the interviews and biographies will be helpful for sparking discussion among your book club members.

What To Do If the Web Site Links Don't Work

In accordance with the instant gratification of the Internet, many sites may be abandoned or changed. Links that don't work are inevitable.

First, you may wish to try a different web browser. Certain media applications may run better in one browser than another.

Second, you may wish to search the title of the webpage in a search engine such as Google.

Third, if the page is part of a magazine or larger Web site, try using that site's internal search.

Finally, you may have luck searching the URL in the Internet Archives, http://www.archive.org.

Alphabetical List of Authors

Jane Austen
Mary Balogh
Jo Beverley
Terri Blackstock aka Terry
    Harrington aka Tracy Hughes
Suzanne Brockmann
Charlotte Brontë and Emily Brontë
Sandra Brown aka Rachel Ryan aka
    Erin St. Claire
Barbara Cartland
Loretta Chase
Catherine Coulter
Jennifer Crusie
Janet Dailey
Jude Deveraux
Eileen Dreyer, aka Kathleen Korbel
Daphne du Maurier
Kathleen Eagle
Christine Feehan
Lori Foster aka L. L. Foster
Roberta Gellis
Rachel Gibson
Heather Graham aka Heather
    Graham Pozzessere aka
    Shannon Drake

Robin Lee Hatcher aka Robin Leigh
Candice Hern
Georgette Heyer
Linda Howard
Judith Ivory
Karin Kallmaker aka Laura
Adams
Lisa Kleypas
Jayne Ann Krentz aka Amanda
    Quick aka Jayne Castle aka
    Stephanie James aka Jayne
    Bentley aka Jayne Taylor aka
    Amanda Glass
Stephanie Laurens
Johanna Lindsey
Cathie Linz
Elizabeth Lowell aka Ann Maxwell
    aka A. E. Maxwell
Debbie Macomber
Judith McNaught
Teresa Medeiros
Kasey Michaels aka Michelle Kasey
Linda Lael Miller
Susan Elizabeth Phillips
Mary Jo Putney aka M. J. Putney

Julia Quinn
Nora Roberts aka J. D. Robb
Sharon Sala aka Dinah McCall
Christina Skye
Bertrice Small

LaVyrle Spencer
Mary Stewart
Anne Stuart
Susan Wiggs
Kathleen E. Woodiwiss

Authors Listed by Romance Subgenre

Contemporary

Terri Blackstock
Suzanne Brockmann
Sandra Brown
Catherine Coulter
Jennifer Crusie
Janet Dailey
Christine Feehan
Lori Foster
Rachel Gibson
Heather Graham
Linda Howard
Karin Kallmaker
Lisa Kleypas
Jayne Ann Krentz
Cathie Linz
Elizabeth Lowell
Debbie Macomber
Dinah McCall
Judith McNaught
Kasey Michaels
Linda Lael Miller
Susan Elizabeth Phillips
Mary Jo Putney
Nora Roberts
Sharon Sala
Susan Wiggs

Romantic Suspense

Terri Blackstock
Suzanne Brockmann
Sandra Brown
Catherine Coulter
Jude Deveraux
Eileen Dreyer
Daphne du Maurier
Kathleen Eagle
Heather Graham
Linda Howard
Elizabeth Lowell
Ann Maxwell
Judith McNaught
Nora Roberts
J. D. Robb
Sharon Sala
Christina Skye
Mary Stewart
Anne Stuart

Category

Sandra Brown
Catherine Coulter
Jennifer Crusie
Janet Dailey
Lori Foster
Kathleen Korbel
Kathleen Eagle
Linda Howard
Jayne Ann Krentz
Cathie Linz
Elizabeth Lowell
Debbie Macomber
Linda Lael Miller
Sharon Sala
LaVyrle Spencer
Anne Stuart

Historical

Mary Balogh
Jo Beverley
Barbara Cartland
Loretta Chase
Catherine Coulter
Jude Deveraux
Shannon Drake
Daphne du Maurier
Kathleen Eagle
Roberta Gellis
Robin Lee Hatcher
Candice Hern
Georgette Heyer
Linda Howard
Judith Ivory
Karin Kallmaker
Lisa Kleypas
Stephanie Laurens
Johanna Lindsey
Amanda Quick
Elizabeth Lowell
Judith McNaught
Teresa Medeiros
Kasey Michaels

Linda Lael Miller
Susan Elizabeth Phillips
Mary Jo Putney
Julia Quinn
Christina Skye
Bertrice Small
LaVyrle Spencer
Mary Stewart
Anne Stuart
Susan Wiggs
Kathleen E. Woodiwiss

Regency

Jane Austen
Mary Balogh
Jo Beverley
Loretta Chase
Catherine Coulter
Candice Hern
Georgette Heyer
Stephanie Laurens
Kasey Michaels
Mary Jo Putney
Julia Quinn

Medieval

Jo Beverley
Jude Deveraux
Roberta Gellis
Elizabeth Lowell
Judith McNaught
Teresa Medeiros
Mary Stewart
Anne Stuart

Western

Johanna Lindsey
Linda Lael Miller

Paranormal

Jayne Castle
Jude Deveraux

Roberta Gellis
Shannon Drake
Christine Feehan
Linda Howard
Karin Kallmaker
Jayne Ann Krentz
Johanna Lindsey
Teresa Medeiros
Linda Lael Miller
Mary Jo Putney
Nora Roberts

Christina Skye
Bertrice Small
Mary Stewart
Anne Stuart

Inspirational

Terri Blackstock
Robin Lee Hatcher
Debbie Macomber

Romance Authors

Jane Austen (1775–1817)

Regency / Historical

Biographical Sketch

Jane Austen is the grandmother, godmother, founder, and creator of the romance novel. Her works are routinely listed as inspiration for many of today's most successful romance authors. All of her novels have been made into movies, often more than once, and the BBC/A&E version of *Pride & Prejudice* is routinely considered a classic by Austen fans. Austen's works are still taught in literature classes on many college campuses and discussed in book clubs around the country.

Born into a genteel family in 1775 in the county of Hampshire, Jane Austen was the seventh of eight children. Her childhood was filled with family and reading. After the death of her father, Jane, her sister Cassandra, and their mother moved several times to be close to family. Finally in 1809, they settled in at Chawton Cottage in Hampshire where Jane lived the remainder of her life. Jane wrote stories to entertain her family but eventually turned to serious novel writing in the 1790s. Two stories were completed before Jane submitted *Sense and Sensibility* to a serial publisher. In 1817 Jane fell ill and died. Her final two novels were published by her brother after her death.

> *It is a truth universally acknowledged that a single man in possession of a good fortune must be in want of a wife.*
>
> Jane Austen
> *Pride and Prejudice*, 1813

Major Works

Novels

Northanger Abbey, 1817
Persuasion, 1817

Emma, 1815
Mansfield Park, 1814
Pride and Prejudice, 1813
Sense and Sensibility, 1811

Novels Based on the Novels of Jane Austen

Austen, Jane and Winters, Ben H. *Sense and Sensibility and Sea Monsters.* Philadelphia, PA: Quirk Books. 2009.

Fowler, Karen Joy. *The Jane Austen Book Club.* New York: Putnam. 2004.

Grahame-Smith, Seth and Austen, Jane. *Pride and Prejudice and Zombies: The Classic Regency Romance, Now with Ultraviolent Zombie Mayhem.* Philadelphia, PA: Quirk Books. 2009.

Rigler, Laurie Viera. *Confessions of a Jane Austen Addict.* New York: Dutton. 2007.

Movies Based on the Novels of Jane Austen

Chadha, Gurinder, director. *Bride and Prejudice,* motion picture. February 11, 2005. Internet Movie Database, http://www.imdb.com/title/tt0361411/. Last visited September 2009.

Heckerling, Amy, director. *Clueless,* motion picture. July 19, 1995. Internet Movie Database, http://www.imdb.com/title/tt0112697/. Last visited September 2009.

Langton, Simon, director. *Pride and Prejudice,* BBC/A&E, made for TV miniseries. January 14, 1996. Internet Movie Database, http://www.imdb.com/title/tt0112130/. Last visited September 2009.

Lee, Ang, director. *Sense and Sensibility,* motion picture. December 13, 1995. Internet Movie Database, http://www.imdb.com/title/tt0114388/. Last visited September 2009.

McGrath, Douglas, director. *Emma,* motion picture. August 2, 1996. Internet Movie Database, http://www.imdb.com/title/tt0116191/. Last visited September 2009.

Wright, Joe, director. *Pride and Prejudice,* motion picture. November 23, 2005. Internet Movie Database, http://www.imdb.com/title/tt0414387/. Last visited September 2009.

Research Sources

For additional research sources please consult your library catalog, the MLA Bibliography or you librarian for assistance. Below is a sample of the resources available.

Encyclopedias and Handbooks

Copeland, Edward and McMaster, Juliet. *The Cambridge Companion to Jane Austen.* New York: Cambridge University Press. 1997.

Kelly, Gary. "Jane Austen." In *Dictionary of Literary Biography: British Romantic Novelist,* 1789–1832. Volume 116. Detroit, MI: Gale Research. 1992.

Olsen, Kirstin. *All Things Austen: An Encyclopedia of Austen's World.* Westport, CT: Greenwood Press. 2005.

Poplawski, Paul. *A Jane Austen Encyclopedia.* Westport, CT: Greenwood Press. 1998.

Biographies and Interviews

Halperin, John. *The Life of Jane Austen.* Baltimore, MD: Johns Hopkins Press. 1996.

Honan, Park. *Jane Austen: Her Life.* New York: St. Marin's Press. 1987.

Nokes, David. *Jane Austen: A Life.* New York: Farrar, Straus and Giroux. 1997.

Shields, Carol. *Jane Austen.* New York: Viking. 2001.

Criticism and Readers' Guides

Bloom, Harold. *Jane Austen.* New York: Chelsea House Publishers. 1986.

Harzewski, Stephanie. *The New Novel of Manners: Chick Lit and Postfeminist Sexual Politics.* PhD Dissertation. University of Pennsylvania. 2006.

Monaghan, David, Hudelet, Ariane and Wiltshire, John. *The Cinematic Jane Austen: Essays on the Filmic Sensibility of the Novels.* Jefferson, NC: McFarland and Company. 2009.

Watt, Ian P. *Jane Austen: A Collection of Critical Essays.* Englewood Cliffs, NJ: Prentice-Hall. 1963.

White, Laura Mooneyham. *Critical Essays on Jane Austen.* New York: G. K. Hall. 1998.

Web Sites

Jane Austen Information Page. http://www.pemberley.com/janeinfo/janeinfo. html. Last visited December 2009. The ultimate fan site; includes bibliography of works related to Austen's novels, annotations to the text of Austen's novels, and an extensive list of links to anything related to Jane Austen.

Jane Austen Society of North America. http://www.jasna.org/. Last visited December 2009. A nonprofit organization to share information about Jane Austen, including a news & notes page, regional groups and meetings, and resources for teachers and students.

Derbyshire Writer's Guild. http://austen.com/. Last visited December 2009. A fan site devoted to the works of Jane Austen, with an extensive compilation of fan fiction, a discussion board, and a list of links.

Mary Balogh (1944–)

Historical / Regency

Biographical Sketch

Mary Balogh (pronounced "Bahlog") was born in Wales and later migrated to Canada after completing her university degree. A two-year teaching contract in Saskatchewan, Canada, turned into a lifetime of love after an unforgettable blind date. Balogh currently lives in Saskatchewan with her husband. After 20 years of teaching she has retired to write full-time.

Her novels closely follow with the "novel of manners" style popularized by Austen and Heyer and are set during the Regency era. Many of her stories contain characters from previous stories, providing readers with an updated look at beloved characters.

Balogh's characters walk a delicate balance by closely following the traditional roles of males and females during the Regency without being so foreign that the modern reader feels that she or he is reading Austen. Balogh also provides very detailed portraits of the time periods, including clothing, food, manners, and daily life.

> *"Show me you are vulnerable, . . . have I hurt you at all? Show me one chink in the armor. Show me that you are not all saint. Show me that you are a man who can feel and suffer."*

Mary Balogh
The Gilded Web, 1989

Major Works

Novels in Series

Huxtable Family

A Secret Affair, 2010
Seducing An Angel, 2009
At Last Comes Marriage, 2009
Then Comes Seduction, 2009
First Comes Marriage, 2009

Simply

Simply Perfect, 2008
Simply Magic, 2007
Simply Love, 2006
Simply Unforgettable, 2005

Bedwyn Family

Slightly Dangerous, 2005
Slightly Sinful, 2004

Slightly Tempted, 2004
Slightly Scandalous, 2003
Slightly Wicked, 2003
Slightly Married, 2003

Web Series

A Promise of Spring, 1990
The Devil's Web, 1990
Web of Love, 1990
The Gilded Web, 1989

Novels

A Summer to Remember, 2002
No Man's Mistress, 2001
More Than a Mistress, 2000
Irresistible, 1998
Thief of Dreams, 1998
The Last Waltz, 1998
Unforgiven, 1998
A Christmas Bride, 1997
Silent Melody, 1997
The Temporary Wife, 1997
Indiscreet, 1997
The Plumed Bonnet, 1996
Truly, 1996
The Famous Heroine, 1996
Heartless, 1995
Lord Carew's Bride, 1995
A Christmas Belle, 1994
Dancing with Clara, 1994
Tempting Harriet, 1994
Dark Angel, 1994
A Precious Jewel, 1993
Courting Julia, 1993
A Counterfeit Betrothal, 1992
The Notorious Rake, 1992

A Christmas Promise, 1992
A Certain Magic, 1991
Snow Angel, 1991
The Secret Pearl, 1991
The Ideal Wife, 1991
Christmas Beau, 1991
The Incurable Matchmaker, 1990
An Unlikely Duchess, 1990
A Daring Masquerade, 1989
A Gift of Daisies, 1989
The Obedient Bride, 1989
Lady with a Black Umbrella, 1989
Secrets of the Heart, 1988
An Unacceptable Offer, 1988
The Ungrateful Governess, 1988
The Wood Nymph, 1987
The Constant Heart, 1987
Gentle Conquest, 1987
Red Rose, 1986
The Trysting Place, 1986
The First Snowdrop, 1986
A Masked Deception, 1985
The Double Wager, 1985
A Chance Encounter, 1985

Research Sources

Encyclopedias and Handbooks

Campbell, P. "Mary Balogh." In *Twentieth-Century Romance and Historical Writers.* Ed. Aruna Vasudevan. 3rd ed. London: St. James Press. 1990. pp. 32–33.

"Mary Balogh." *Literature Resource Center.* (subscription database). 2009. http://galenet.galegroup.com/. Last visited June 2009.

Biographies and Interviews

"At the Back Fence, Issue #199." *All About Romance.* April 15, 2005. http://www.likesbooks.com/199.html#balogh. Last visited April 2009.

"At the Back Fence, Issue #147." *All About Romance.* October 15, 2002. http://www.likesbooks.com/147.html#balogh. Last visited April 2009.

At the Back Fence, Issue #115." *All About Romance.* April 15, 2001. http://www.likesbooks.com/115.html#balogh. Last visited April 2009.

"At the Back Fence, Issue #96." *All About Romance.* June 1, 2000. http://www.likesbooks.com/96.html#balogh. Last visited April 2009.

Balogh, Mary. "Do It Passionately or Not at All." In *North American Romance Writers.* Ed. Kay Mussell and Johanna Tunon. London: Scarecrow Press. 1999. pp. 19–28.

Coleman, Sandy. Writer's Corner: Mary Balogh. *All About Romance.* September 13, 2007. http://www.likesbooks.com/balogh2007.html. Last visited September 2009.

Dyer, Lucinda. "Musings on Muses." *Publisher's Weekly,* Volume 251, Issue 46, November 15, 2004. pp. 34–35.

Frederick, Heather Vogel. "Mary Balogh: Two Men in her Life." *Publishers Weekly,* Volume 247, Issue 28, July 10, 2000. p. 32.

"Mary Balogh: Regency Romance's Shining Star." *All About Romance.* February 12, 2008. http://www.likesbooks.com/balogh.html. Last visited April 2009.

Ramsdell, Kristin and Bette-Lee Fox. "Q&A: Mary Balogh." *Library Journal,* Volume 134, Issue 3, 2009. p. 90.

Smith, Caliboorne. "Stars in the Ascendent: On Time, and Often Early." *Publishers Weekly,* Volume 250, Issue 27, July 7, 2003. pp. 37–45.

Web Site

Mary Balogh Web site. http://www.marybalogh.com/. Last visited December 2009. The official Web site of Mary Balogh, with information about the author, a list of her upcoming books, and excerpts from previously published novels.

Jo Beverley (1947–)

Historical / Regency / Georgian / Medieval

Biographical Sketch

Jo Beverley, who is inspired by Georgette Heyer, writes medieval romances, Regency romances, romances that take place in the Georgian period preceding the Regency, as well as science fiction novellas. Beverley's popular Rogues series takes place during the Regency with characters trying to fit into culture of the *ton*, the aristocracy. Her female characters are true to the time period while her male characters are always strong but never overbearing.

Beverley was born in England in 1947, immigrated to Canada with her husband. Beverley completed her degree in English from Keele University in Staffordshire, England. Medieval romances are her first love, but it was a publication of a Regency novel that started her writing career. Beverley is a multi-winner of the RITA award and a member of the Romance Writers of America Hall of Fame.

It isn't often a man hears a cursing nun.

Robin Fitzvitry, Earl of Huntersdown was finishing his meal at a table by the window and thus had an excellent view of the woman out in the coach yard. There could be no doubt. She was muttering curses and she was a nun.

Jo Beverley
A Lady's Secret, 2008

Major Works

Novels in Series

The Malloren World

The Secret Duke, 2010	*Devilish*, 2000
The Secret Wedding, 2009	*Secrets of the Night*, 1999
A Lady's Secret, 2008	*Something Wicked*, 1997
A Most Unsuitable Man, 2005	*Tempting Fortune*, 1995
Winter Fire, 2003	*My Lady Notorious*, 1993

The Company of Rogues

Lady Beware, 2007	*The Dragon's Bride*, 2001
To Rescue a Rogue, 2006	*Dangerous Joy*, 1995
The Rogue's Return, 2006	*Forbidden*, 1994
Skylark, 2004	*Christmas Angel*, 1992
St. Raven, 2003	*An Unwilling Bride*, 1992
Hazard, 2002	*An Arranged Marriage*, 1991

Novels

The Secret Duke, 2010	*The Rogue's Return*, 2006
The Secret Wedding, 2009	*A Most Unsuitable Man*, 2005
A Lady's Secret, 2008	*Skylark*, 2004
Lady Beware, 2007	*Winter Fire*, 2003
To Rescue a Rogue, 2006	*St. Raven*, 2003

Hazard, 2002
The Dragons Bride, 2001
The Devil's Heiress, 2001
Devilish, 2000
Secrets of the Night, 1999
Lord of Midnight, 1998
Forbidden Magic, 1998
Something Wicked, 1997
The Shattered Rose, 1996
Tempting Fortune, 1995
Dangerous Joy, 1995
Forbidden, 1994

Deirdre and Don Juan, 1993
Dark Champion, 1993
My Lady Notorious, 1993
An Unwilling Bride, 1992
Christmas Angel, 1992
Lord of My Heart, 1992
An Arranged Marriage, 1991
Emily and the Dark Angel, 1991
The Fortune Hunter, 1991
Lord Wraybourne's Betrothed, 1990
The Stolen Bride, 1990
The Stanforth Secrets, 1989

Other Works

"Historical Fiction." *The Writer,* Volume 118, Issue 7, July 2005. pp. 36–40.

"An Honorable Profession: The Romance Writer and Her Characters." In *North American Romance Writers.* Ed. Kay Mussell and Johanna Tunon. London: Scarecrow Press. 1999. pp. 29–36.

"Write Byte: The Norman Conquest: 1050–1120." *All About Romance.* 1998. http://www.likesbooks.com/medevil1.html. Last visited June 2009.

"Write Byte: The Georgian Age: 1714–1830." *All About Romance.* 1998. http://www.likesbooks.com/georgian.html. Last visited June 2009.

"Write Byte: Authors and the Internet," *All About Romance.* December 13, 2000. http://www.likesbooks.com/wb26.html. Last visited June 2009.

Research Sources

Encyclopedias and Handbooks

"Jo Beverley." *Literature Resource Center.* (subscription database). 2009. http://galenet.galegroup.com/. Last visited June 2009.

Biographies and Interviews

"A Quickie from Jo Beverley." *All About Romance.* http://www.likesbooks. com/quickie6.html. Last visited June 2009.

"At the Back Fence, Issue #147."*All About Romance.* October 15, 2002. http://www.likesbooks.com/147.html#jo. Last visited June 2009.

"At the Back Fence, Issue #211." *All About Romance.* November 21, 2005. http://www.likesbooks.com/211.html#jo. Last visited June 2009.

"Behind the Pen of . . . Jo Beverley" *All About Romance.* 1996. http://www. likesbooks.com/beverley.html. Last visited June 2009.

Bolton, Kathleen. "Author Interview: Jo Beverley, Part One." *Writer Unboxed.* March 13, 2009. http://writerunboxed.com/2009/03/13/author-interview-jo-beverley-part-one/. Last visited June 2009.

Bolton, Kathleen. "Author Interview: Jo Beverley, Part Two." *Writer Unboxed.* March 20, 2009. http://writerunboxed.com/2009/03/20/author-interview-jo-beverley-part-two/. Last visited June 2009.

Dyer, Lucinda. "Musings on Muses." *Publisher's Weekly,* Volume 251, Issue 46, November 15, 2004. pp. 34–35.

Jaegly, Peggy. "Jo Beverley." *Romantic Hearts: A Personal Reference for Romance Readers.* 3rd ed. Lanham, MD: Scarecrow Press. 1997. pp. 4–5.

Kissia. "Secrets of the Author: Jo Beverley on the Mallorens and Writing." *Subversion Romance: Celebrating Women's Fiction.* http://www.subversionromance.com/articles/secrets-of-the-author/. Last visited June 2009.

Putney, Mary Jo. "Lady Beware!: A Chat with Jo Beverley." *Word Wenches blog.* May 29, 2007. http://wordwenches.typepad.com/word_wenches/2007/05/lady_beware_a_c.html. Last visited June 2009.

Web Site

Jo Beverley Web site. http://www.jobeverley.com. Last visited December 2009. The official Web site of Jo Beverley contains information about the author with pictures, a complete book list with excerpts to some of her works, and a list of upcoming book signings.

Terri Blackstock / Terry Harrington / Tracy Hughes (1957–)

Contemporary / Inspirational / Romantic Suspense / Category

Biographical Sketch

Terri Blackstock wrote her early romance novels under the name Terry Herrington and the pseudonym Tracy Hughes. In 1981 Blackstock received a bachelor's degree in English from Northeast Louisiana University. Blackstock's first marriage ended in 1990 and she married her second husband Ken in 1992. After the end of her first marriage, Blackstock felt called to write inspirational Christian romances and does not promote or recommend her earlier works.

Blackstock's most successful inspirational titles are her romantic suspense works featuring strong plots. Her characters find the crisis in the novel leads them to a stronger faith in God and a stronger relationship with each other.

As she leaped over it, the gun fired again. Hot wind whizzed past her calf, and she fell over the bike, flipping quickly onto her back to defend herself. She screamed again as the killer came closer, aiming for her chest.

Terri Blackstock
Dawn's Light, 2009

Major Works

Novels in Series by Terri Blackstock

The Restoration

Dawn's Light, 2009
True Light, 2007
Night Light, 2006
Last Light, 2005

Cape Refuge

Breaker's Reef, 2005
River's Edge, 2004
Southern Storm, 2003
Cape Refuge, 2002

Newpointe 911

Line of Duty, 2003
Trial by Fire, 2000
Word of Honor, 1999
Shadow of Doubt, 1998
Private Justice, 1998

The Second Chances

When Dreams Cross, 2000
Never Again Good-Bye, 2000
Broken Wings, 2000
Blind Trust, 1998

Sun Coast Chronicles

Justifiable Means, 1998
Presumption of Guilt, 1997
Ulterior Motives, 1996
Evidence of Mercy, 1995

Novels by Terri Blackstock

Predator, 2010
Intervention, 2009
Double Minds, 2009
The Heart Reader of Franklin High, 2009
Sweet Delights, 2008

Covenant Child, 2002
The Gifted, 2002
Seaside, 2001
Emerald Windows, 2001
The Listener, 2000

Collaborations by Terri Blackstock

With Beverly LaHaye

Season of Blessings, 2003
Times and Seasons, 2002
Seasons Under Heaven, 2001
Showers in Season, 2000

Novels by Terri Herrington

Winner Take All, 1995
One Good Man, 1993

Silena, 1993
Her Father's Daughter, 1991

Category Novels by Terri Herrington

Candlelight Ecstasy Romance

Ticket to a Fantasy, #500, 1987
Stolen Moments, #489, 1987
Head Over Heels, #464, 1986
A Secret Stirring, #438, 1986

Other Category Novels by Terri Herrington

Flashback, Silhouette Shadows #7, 1993
Wife Wanted, Silhouette Romance #561, 1988
Tangled Triumphs, Silhouette Romance #509, 1987
Tender Betrayer, Candlelight Ecstasy Supreme #136, 1986

Novels by Tracy Hughes

Harlequin Super Romance

Daniel, #706, 1996
Catch a Falling Star, #623, 1994
The Princess and the Pauper, #594, 1994
While Lies & Alibis, #399, 1990
Emerald Windows, #381, 1989
Jo, #342, 1989
Above the Clouds, #304, 1988

Harlequin American Romance

To Heaven and Back, #578, 1995
Heaven Knows, #542, 1994
Delta Dust, #502, 1993
Sand Man, #455, 1992
Father Knows Best, #438, 1992
Second Chances, #410, 1991
Honorbound, #381, 1991

Harlequin Romance

Impressions, #2792, 1986
Quiet Lightning, #2744, 1986

Other Works

Soul Restoration: Hope for the Weary, 2005

Research Sources

Encyclopedias and Handbooks

"Terri Blackstock." *Literature Resource Center.* (subscription database). 2003. http://galenet.galegroup.com/. Last visited June 2009.

Biographies and Interviews

Abbot, Krista. "Terri Blackstock Interview." *Destiny Talk Radio.* October 3, 2009. http://www.blogtalkradio.com/destinytalkradio/blog/2009/10/03/terri-blackstock-interview. Last visited December 2009.

Cuevas, Laci. "An Interview with Terri Blackstock." *Mississippi Writers & Musicians.* February 5, 2003. http://www.mswritersandmusicians.com/writers/terri-blackstock.html. Last visited December 2009.

Darlington, C. J. " Terri Blackstock Interview." *Title Trakk.* http://www.titletrakk.com/author-interviews/terri-blackstock-interview.htm. Last visited December 2009.

George, Tim. "An Interview with Terri Blackstock." *Unveiled.* August 13, 2009. http://www.tegeorge.com/unveiled/?p=336. Last visited December 2009.

Mulligan, Ane. "Author Interview—Terri Blackstock." *Novel Journey.* June 20, 2007. http://noveljourney.blogspot.com/2007/06/author-interview-terri-blackstock.html. Last visited December 2009.

"Our Interview with Terri Blackstock." *Christian Book.com.* http://www.christianbook.com/Christian/Books/cms_content?page=787748&event=CF. Last visited December 2009.

Sleeman, Susan. "Terri Blackstock Interview with Susan Sleeman." *The Suspense Zone.* http://www.thesuspensezone.com/InterviewTerriBlackstock.html/. Last visited December 2009.

Web Site

Terri Blackstock Best Selling Author. http://www.terriblackstock.com. Last visited December 2009. Terri Blackstock's official webpage; includes biographical information, a backlist of her Chrisitian novels, a journal, and an FAQ.

Suzanne Brockmann (1960–)

Contemporary / Romantic Suspense

Biographical Sketch

Brockmann's novels are suspenseful, realistic, and sometimes even violent. Characters die, and not just the bad guys. The characters also use real language that demonstrates how real people react in stressful situations. There is a lot of action, but it never overwhelms the romance and there is usually more than one romance in the story. Brockmann employs a wonderful use of history that enriches her stories and adds an additional level of suspense, an example being a secondary story line involving a World

War II setting in several of her *Troubleshooter* novels. Brockmann's *Silhouette Intimate Moment* novel, *Harvard's Education,* featured an African American hero, which was only the second time that Silhouette had published a category novel featuring an African American hero. In the novel *All Through the Night,* Brockmann elevated the gay best-friend character to a starring role giving him his own happy ending. Brockman is one of the few romance authors to carry the romance of her characters through multiple novels.

Brockmann was born in New Jersey and attended Boston University, but did not graduate. She began her writing career creating screenplays and TV scripts, but none made it to the screen. To make her work more marketable, Brockmann made the move from screenwriting to romance.

With her focus on Navy Seals, Ms. Brockmann's novels feature strong men and the strong women who fight with them. Many of the female characters are also involved in dangerous careers such as the U.S. military, the FBI, or other law enforcement agencies. Because of this combination of strong characters and fast-paced action, Brockmann's novels stand out in the romance genre.

. . . it was Alyssa Locke.

*She'd handcuffed him to her before he could even tell his feet to run.
"Hey, Sam. Nice tie," she said, then yanked him through the back door.*

Suzanne Brockmann
Gone Too Far, 2003

Major Works

Novels in Series

Troubleshooters

Hot Pursuit, 2009
Dark of Night, 2009
Into the Fire, 2008
All Through the Night, 2007
Force of Nature, 2007
Into the Storm, 2006
Breaking Point, 2005
Hot Target, 2004

Flashpoint, 2004
Gone Too Far, 2003
Into the Night, 2002
Out of Control, 2002
Over the Edge, 2001
The Defiant Hero, 2001
The Unsung Hero, 2000

Novels

Infamous, 2010
Bodyguard, 1999
Heart Throb, 1999
Embraced by Love, 1995

Category Novels

Silhouette Intimate Moments Titles

Night Watch, #1243, 2003
Letter's to Kelly, #1213, 2003
Taylor's Temptation, #1087,
     2001
Get Lucky, #991, 2000
Identity Unknown, #974, 2000
Undercover Princess, #968, 1999
The Admiral's Bride, #962, 1999
It Came Upon a Midnight Clear, #896,
     1998

Harvard's Education, #884, 1998
Everyday Average Jones, #872, 1998
Love With the Proper Stranger, #831,
     1998
Frisco's Kid, #759, 1997
Forever Blue, #742, 1996
Prince Joe, #720, 1996
A Man to Die For, #681, 1995
Not Without Risk, #647, 1995
Hero Under Cover, #575, 1994

Bantam Loveswept Titles

Body Language, #889, 1998
Freedom's Price, #873, 1998
Time Enough for Love, #858, 1997
Ladies Man, #840, 1997
Stand-In Groom, #840, 1997
Forbidden, #832, 1997
Otherwise Engages, #824, 1997
The Kissing Game, #817, 1996
Kiss and Tell, #787, 1996

Other Category Titles

Scenes of Passion, Silhouette Desire #1519, 2003
Give me Liberty, Precious Gems #86, 1997
No Ordinary Man, Harlequin Intrigue #365, 1996
Future Perfect, Meteor Kismet #168, 1993

Other Works

Reader's Guide to the Troubleshooter Series. http://www.randomhouse.com/
     rhpg/PDF/IntoTheStorm_Sampler.pdf.
"Write Byte: The Company that Sells You Series Romance." All About Ro-
     mance. April 15, 2002. http://www.likesbooks.com/137a.html. Last vis-
     ited June 2009.
"Write Byte: What's It All About, Alpha? Or The Up Side of Dark Heroes."
     All About Romance. http://www.likesbooks.com/alpha.html. Last visited
     June 2009.

Research Sources

Encyclopedias and Reference Sources

Charles, John. "Suzanne Brockmann." In *Romance Today: An A-To-Z Guide to Contemporary American Romance Writers.* Ed. John Charles and Shelley Mosley. Westport, CT: Greenwood. 2007. pp. 37–40.

"Suzanne Brockmann." *Literature Resource Center.* (subscription database). 2009. http://galenet.galegroup.com/. Last visited June 2009.

Biographies and Interviews

Mason, Jean. "Meet Author Suzanne Brockmann." *The Romance Reader.* November 28, 2000. http://www.theromancereader.com/brockmann. html. Last visited June 2009.

Terrones, Claudia. "A Chat with Suzanne Brockmann." *All About Romance.* February 19, 2001. http://www.likesbooks.com/suzannebrockmann.html. Last visited June 2009.

Vido, Jennifer. "Meet the Author: Featuring Jen's Jewels." February 1, 2009. http://www.hcplonline.info/readers/archive_meet_the_author/meetthe author_feb09_01.htm. Last visited June 2009.

Ward, Jean Marie. "Suzanne Brockmann: SEAL-ed with a Kiss." *Crescent Blues e-Magazine,* Volume 5, Issue 6, http://www.crescentblues.com/ 5_3issue/int_brockmann.shtml. Last visited December 2009.

White, Claire E. "A Conversation with Suzanne Brockmann." *Writers Write Web site.* February 1, 2005, http://www.writerswrite.com/. Last visited June 2009.

Criticism and Readers' Guides

Frantz, Sarah S. G. "I've Tried my Entire Life to be a Good Man: Suzanne Brockmann's Sam Starrett, Ideal Romance Hero. In *Women Constructing Men: Female Novelists and Their Male Characters,* 1750–2000. Ed. Sarah S. G. Frantz and Katharina Rennhak. Lanham, MD: Lexington. 2009.

Frantz, Sarah S. G. "Suzanne Brockmann." *Teaching American Literature: A Journal of Theory and Practice,* Volume 2, Issue 2–3, Spring–Summer 2008.

Web Sites

Suzanne Brockmann's home page. http://www.suzannebrockmann.com/. Last visited January 2010. The official Web site for Suzanne Brockmann; contains links to upcoming books, backlist and excerpts and a blog.

If You Like Suzanne Brockmann

Suzanne Brockmann writes action, adventure, and romantic suspense romance novels. Her stories feature military men of action who find love in unexpected places. In turn, her heroines are as tough as the heroes, with emotional scars much like those possessed by heroes in other romance novels. Fast-paced action and smart dialogue make a Brockman novel a fun read.

You May Like

Linda Howard

Linda Howard's novels feature male heroes who are emotionally scarred and have to learn to trust in love. Due to the hero's fear of love, he often treats the heroine cruelly and the heroines in a Howard novel generally prove to be stronger than the heroes. Howard's stories are tight, emotional, and some of the best romantic suspense stories published.

Nora Roberts Writing as J. D. Robb

J. D. Robb writes futuristic and romantic suspense novels. Her stories feature Eve Dallas as a homicide detective who, along with her husband Roarke, solve the mystery every time. Witty dialogue and fast-paced action make any Robb (or Roberts book for that matter) an enjoyable read.

Sharon Sala

Sharon Sala writes gritty, realistic, romantic suspense stories that demonstrate that love can exist in a dangerous world. Her characters, all of whom have a core belief in God, give the stories depth and strong appeal and her heroines are flawed but strong.

Christina Skye

Skye's stories are complex and occasionally violent. The heroines may be unconventional with unique skills. The heroes are strong and protective even if they aren't sure about love. Skye's strength is the dialogue of the character driven stories. In the Draycott Abbey series, a witty ghost adds humor and a touch of the paranormal.

Charlotte Brontë (1816–1855) and Emily Brontë (1818–1848)

Romantic Suspense

Biographical Sketch

While the Brontë sister's received little critical or financial success during their lifetimes, their major works continue to fascinate readers. *Wuthering Heights* and *Jane Eyre* are wonderful examples of romantic suspense novels that have been identified as Gothic stories. Both novels were made into motion pictures, with Orson Welles and Joan Fontaine playing Rochester and

Jane in one of the classic versions of *Jane Eyre* and Laurence Olivier and Merle Oberone portraying Cathy and Heathcliff in an equally classic version of *Wuthering Heights*.

Charlotte and Emily Brontë were born into a family of writers. Their father, a clergyman, published fiction and poetry the same year as Emily's birth. Like all the children of the Reverend Brontë, the sisters were educated at private schools and then became teachers themselves. Emily was also briefly a governess in a private household. Both sisters traveled to Belgium to gain experience as teachers in the hopes of setting up their own school. While the school did not happen, Charlotte, Emily, and their sister Anne began writing, first poetry, and then longer stories. During Charlotte's lifetime, her mother and all her siblings, including Emily passed away. Emily died of tuberculosis or more commonly called "consumption" at that time. Charlotte died one year after her marriage to Reverend Arthur Bell Nichols, also of tuberculosis.

Yesterday afternoon set in misty and cold. I had half a mind to spend it by my study fire, instead of wading through heath and mud to Wuthering Heights.

Emily Brontë
Wuthering Heights, 1847

I am no bird; and no net ensnares me; I am a free human being with an independent will.

Charlotte Brontë
Jane Eyre, 1847

Major Works

Novels by Charlotte Bronte

The Professor: A Tale, 1857
Villette, 1853
Shirley: A Tale, 1849
Jane Eyre: An Autobiography, 1847

Novels by Emily Bronte

Wuthering Heights: A Novel, 1847
Poems by Currer, Ellis and Acton Bell, 1846

Other Works

Poems by Currer, Ellis and Acton Bell, 1846 (*poems by various family members*)

Works Based on the Novels of Charlotte Brontë and Emily Brontë

Stevenson, Robert, director. *Jane Eyre,* motion picture. April 7, 1944. Internet Movie Database, http://www.imdb.com/title/tt0036969/. Last visited September 2009.

Wyler, William, director. *Wuthering Heights,* motion picture. April 7, 1939. Internet Movie Database, http://www.imdb.com/title/tt0032145/. Last visited September 2009.

Research Sources

For additional research sources please consult your library catalog, the MLA Bibliography or your librarian for assistance. Below is a sample of the resources available.

Encyclopedias and Handbooks

Barnard, Robert and Barnard, Louise. *A Brontë Encyclopedia.* Oxford, England: Blackwell Publishers. 2007.

Taylor, Susan, Ed. *Dictionary of Literary Biography: The Brontës: A Documentary Volume,* Volume 340. Detroit, MI: Gale Cengage Learning. 2008.

Biographies and Interviews

Bloom, Harold. *The Brontës.* New York: Chelsea House Publishers. 1987.

Gregor, Ian. *The Brontës: A Collection of Critical Essays.* Englewood Cliffs, NJ: Prentice-Hall Publishers. 1970.

Lydall, Gordon. *Charlotte Brontë: A Passionate Life.* New York: W. W. Norton. 1995.

Winnifrith, Tom. The Brontës and Their Background: Romance and Reality. London: Macmillan Publishers. 1973.

Criticism and Readers' Guides

DuVal, Katherine Niell. *The Quiet Heretics: Religion and the Craft of the Brontë Sisters.* PhD Dissertation. University of Arkansas. 1991.

Lee, Jin Ok. *Female Desire and Community in Charlotte Bronte's Works.* PhD Dissertation. New York University. 1997.

Stoneman. Patsy. "The Brontë Legacy: Jane Eyre and Wuthering Heights as Romance Archetypes." *Rivista di Studi Vittoriani,* Volume 5. 1998. pp. 5–24.

Web Sites

Brontë Parsonage Museum & Brontë Society. http://www.bronte.info/. Last visited December 2009. Includes biographical information about the Brontë sisters, educational workshops, an online library catalog of works related to the Brontës, and a blog.

Brussels Brontë Group. http://www.thebrusselsbrontegroup.org/. Last visited December 2009. A Web site devoted to Brontë scholars and fans from Belgium and the Netherlands. Includes a list of group events, a photo gallery with maps and old prints, and a blog.

Sandra Brown / Rachel Ryan / Erin St. Claire (1948–)

Romantic Suspense / Contemporary / Category

Biographical Sketch

Sandra Brown's happy, suburban mom and grandmother lifestyle is a far cry from her fast- paced, occasionally violent, romantic suspense novels. Brown grew up in Waco, Texas, and majored in English at Texas Christian University. Before becoming a full-time writer, she worked in television as a weather-girl and a freelance reporter on *PM Magazine.* Happily married in 1968, she began writing in 1981 while her children were in school.

Brown's books feature current issues, but the characters and plot lines are definitely her own. As one of the many authors who began in series romances, Brown then moved on to longer stories with a more mainstream fiction focus. Her novel *French Silk,* published in 1992, was adapted for a "made for TV" movie, making Brown one of the few contemporary romance authors to have her work translated onto the screen. In 1998, Brown received the prestigious Romance Writers of America Lifetime Achievement Award.

> *They kissed in the balmy twilight. Several blocks away, a saxophone bleated out the blues. Someone living nearby was cooking with file and cayenne pepper. The spicy aromas permeated the air.*
>
> Sandra Brown
> *French Silk,* 1992

Major Works

Novels in Series

Coleman Family Saga

Sunset Embrace, 1985
Another Dawn, 1985

Tyler Family Saga Series

Texas! Sage, 1991
Texas! Chase, 1991
Texas! Lucky, 1990

Novels by Sandra Brown

Tough Customer, 2010
Rainwater, 2009
Smash Cut, 2009
Smoke Screen, 2008
Play Dirty, 2007
Ricochet, 2006
Chill Factor, 2005
White Hot, 2004
Hello, Darkness, 2003
The Crush, 2002
Envy, 2001
Standoff, 2000
The Switch, 2000
The Alibi, 1999

Unspeakable, 1998
Fat Tuesday, 1997
Exclusive, 1996
The Witness, 1995
Charade, 1994
Where There's Smoke, 1993
French Silk, 1992
Shadows of Yesterday, 1992 (originally published as *Relentless Desire,* 1983)
Breath of Scandal, 1991
Mirror Image, 1990
Best Kept Secrets, 1989
Slow Heat in Heaven, 1988

Loveswept Category Novels by Sandra Brown

A Whole New Light, #366, 1989
Temperatures Rising, #336, 1989
Long Time Coming, #300, 1988
Hawk O'Toole's Hostage, #263, 1988
Adam's Fall #252, 1988
Tidings of Great Joy, #229, 1987
Fanta C, #217, 1987
Demon Rumm, #197, 1987
Sunny Chandler's Return, #185, 1987

22 Indigo Place #154, 1986
The Rana Look, #136, 1986
Riley in the Morning, #115, 1985
Thursday's Child, #79, 1985
In a Class by Itself, #66, 1984
Send No Flowers, #51, 1984
Breakfast in Bed, #22, 1983
Heaven's Price, #1, 1983

Other Category Novels by Sandra Brown

Tempest in Eden, Second Chance at Love #164, 1983
Temptations Kiss, Second Chance at Love #137, 1983
Relentless Desire, Second Chance at Love #106, 1983
Tomorrow's Promise, Harlequin American Romance #1, 1983

Category Novels by Rachel Ryan

Candlelight Ecstasy Romance

Prime Time, #151, 1983
A Treasure Worth Seeking, #59, 1982
Eloquent Silence, #49, 1982
Love Beyond Reason, #29, 1981
Love's Encore, #21, 1981

Category Novels by Erin St. Claire

Silhouette Desire

The Thrill of Victory, #488, 1989
Words of Silk, #139, 1984
A Kiss Remembered #73, 1983
Seduction by Design, 41, 1983
Not Even for Love, #7, 1982

Silhouette Intimate Moments

Two Alone, #213, 1987
The Devil's Own, #180, 1987
Honor Bound, #144, 1986
Above and Beyond, #133, 1986
Led Astray, #120, 1985
Tiger Prince, #112, 1985
Sweet Anger, #93, 1985
Bittersweet Rain, #76, 1984
A Secret Splendor, #29, 1983

Novels by Laura Jordan

Hidden Fires, 1982
The Silken Web, 1982

Other Works

"The Risk of Seduction and the Seduction of Risk." In *Dangerous Men & Adventurous Women: Romance Writers on the Appeal of Romance.* Ed. Jayne Ann Krentz. Philadelphia: University of Pennsylvania Press. 1992. pp. 179–185.

Films Made from Novels

Nosseck, Noel, director. *French Silk,* ABC TV Movie of the Week. January 23, 1994. Internet Movie Database, http://www.imdb.com/title/tt0109841/. Last visited July 2009.

Research Sources

Encyclopedias and Handbooks

"Sandra Brown." *Literature Resource Center.* (subscription database). 2009. http://galenet.galegroup.com/. Last visited June 2009.
Kemp, Barbara. "Sandra Brown." In *Twentieth-Century Romance and Historical Writers.* Ed. Aruna Vasudevan. 3rd ed. London: St. James Press. 1990. pp. 84–86.

Biographies and Interviews

Arnold, Martin. "With Romance Behind Them." *New York Times.* September 16, 1999. p. E3. http://www.nytimes.com/1999/09/16/books/making-books-with-romance-behind-them.html?pagewanted=1. Last visited January 2010.

"Author Talk: Sandra Brown." *BookReporter.com.* August 2004. http://www.bookreporter.com/authors/au-brown-sandra.asp. Last visited June 2009.

Bearden, Michele. "Sandra Brown: Suburban Mom and Prolific Bestseller." *Publisher's Weekly,* Volume 242, Issue 28, July 10, 1995. pp. 39.

Foege, Alec and Haederle, Michael. "Texas Tornado." *People,* Volume 50, Issue 10, September 21, 1998. pp 81–82.

Frumkes, Lewis. "Sandra Brown Interview." *Lewis Burke Frumkes Radio Show.* Audio interview. August 31, 2008. http://jonathanmaberry.com/a-conversation-with-sandra-brown. Last visited July 2009

Guiley, Rosemary. "Sandra Brown." *Love Lines: A Romance Reader's Guide to Printed Pleasures.* New York: Facts on File Publications. 1983. pp. 197–198.

Havens, Candace. "Candace Haven Interviews Sandra Brown." *Candy's Inside Books: A Look at Books, Authors, and Movie Events.* August 10, 2008. http://freshfiction.com/page.php?id=1172. Last visited July 2009.

Hollandsworth, Skip. "The Woman on Top: A Few Things in Life are Certain—Turkeys Will Be Carved Every Fall, Taxes Will Be Due Every Spring, and Sandra Brown Will Publish a New Best-Seller Every Summer." *Texas Monthly.* August 2007.

Homes, Gina. "Interview with NYT Best-Selling Novelist, Sandra Brown." *Novel Journey.* August 28, 2007. http://noveljourney.blogspot.com/2007/08/interview-with-nyt-best-selling.html. Last visited July 2009.

MaBerry, Jonathan. "Conversation with Sandra Brown." *Jonathan Maberry's Big, Scary Blog: A Conversation about Books, Writing, Publishing and Everything in Between.* April 22, 2009. http://jonathanmaberry.com/a-conversation-with-sandra-brown. Last visited July 2009.

Mitchell, Sandy. "An Interview with Sandra Brown: Bestselling Mystery Author Talks about Writing, Reading, and Life." *Suite 101.com.* August 14, 2007. http://mysterycrimefiction.suite101.com/article.cfm/an_interview_with_sandra_brown/. Last visited July 2009.

Thompson, Bill. "Sandra Brown on the Writer's Craft." Bill Thompson's Eye on Books. http://www.eyeonbooks.com/icp.php?authID=1287. Last visited July 2009.

"Sandra Brown Chat Transcript." *Washington Post.* September 22, 2005. http://www.washingtonpost.com/wp-dyn/content/discussion/2005/09/04/DI2005090400843.html. Last visited July 2009.

Criticism and Readers' Guides

Rapp, Adrian, Dodgen, Lynda and Kaler, Anne K. "A Romance Writer Gets Away with Murder." *Clues: A Journal of Detection,* Volume 21, Issue 1, Spring–Summer 2000. pp. 17–21.

Web Site

Sandra Brown. http://www.sandrabrown.net/. Last visited December 2009. The official home page of Sandra Brown; includes information about published and forthcoming books, an FAQ, and photos of Brown and her family.

Barbara Cartland (1901–2000)

Historical / Regency

Biographical Sketch

Barbara Cartland is one of the most prolific authors of all time. Born in Warwickshire County in England, she attended finishing school and wrote her first novel at the age of 21. She married her first husband, Alexander Mc-Corquodale, in 1927 and divorced him in 1932. In 1936, Cartland married his cousin Hugh McCorquodale and they remained happily married until Hugh's death in 1963. Cartland had three children.

In 1950, Cartland bought Camfield Place, the 1867 manor where Beatrix Potter wrote *The Tale of Peter Rabbit.* Once at Camfield Place, Cartland continued her rigorous schedule of novel production. She did not write out or type manuscripts; instead she dictated her stories to a rapidly typing secretary. Tape recordings were used as backups. In 1991, Cartland was made a Dame of the British Empire. Besides writing, Cartland was active in the health food movement of the 1960s and 1970s and in politics. Cartland's daughter, Raine, married the 8th Earl of Spencer in 1975 becoming the Countess Spencer and the stepmother of the future Princess of Wales, Diana.

Cartland's stories were standard romance of the time. Young, virginal heroine meets handsome, rich man, conflict ensues, and then they proceed to the happily ever after. She resisted the movement toward sexier works in the 1970s, keeping the sex for married couples only. At the time of Cartland's death, 150 completed but unpublished novels were found, more than enough to keep new Cartland novels available for a very long time.

> *"She said in the ingenuous manner which hides her Machiavellian brain: 'I think, Marchioness, we must find the Duke of Doncaster a wife!'"*
>
> Barbara Cartland
> *The Incredible Honeymoon,* 1976

Major Works

Below is a selection of the more than 700 novels published by Barbara Cartland. An extensive list of the works of Barbara Cartland is available at the Fantastic Fiction Web site http://www.fantasticfiction.co.uk/c/barbara-cartland/.

A Change of Heart, 2009	*Love in the Highlands,* 2004
Ruled by Love, 2009	*The Lady and the Highwayman,* 2001

Enchanted, 1998
Apocalypse of the Heart, 1995
The Duke's Dilemma, 1994
A Kiss in Rome, 1992
Royal Lovers, 1989
Count the Stars, 1986
Island Masquerade, 1985
Love Comes West, 1984
Gypsy Magic, 1983
The Call of the Highlands, 1982
A Kiss of Silk, 1980
Way of an Eagle, 1979
The Saint and the Sinner, 1978
Karma of Love, 1974
Wicked Marquis, 1973
Stars in My Heart, 1971
Love on the Run, 1969
The Runaway Heart, 1967
The Fire of Love, 1964
Wings of Love, 1962
Sweet Adventure, 1957
The Captive Heart, 1956
Love Me For Ever, 1953
The Knave of Hearts, 1950
The Little Pretender, 1950
A Hazard of Hearts, 1949
No Heart is Free, 1948
Again This Rapture, 1947

If We Will, 1947
The Dream Within, 1947
Against the Stream, 1946
Hidden Heart, 1946
Out of Reach, 1945
The Dark Stream, 1944
Open Wings, 1942
Now Rough, Now Smooth, 1941
Stolen Halo, 1940
The Black Panther, 1939
Bitter Winds of Love, 1938
But Never Free, 1937
Dangerous Experiment, 1936
First Class, Lady, 1935
A Beggar Wished, 1934
Not Love Alone, 1933
Virgin in Mayfair, 1932
Sweet Punishment, 1931
If the Tree is Saved, 1929
Sawdust, 1929
Jigsaw, 1925
Other Works
I Reach for the Stars: An Autobiography,
    1994
I Seek the Miraculous, 1978
We Danced All Night, 1970
I Search for Rainbows, 1969

Research Sources

Biographies and Interviews

Gonazlez Jr., Arturo F. "Guess Who Writes 70,000 Words a Week, Publishes 24 Books a Year, and Says 'Me Tarzan, You Jane' Works Best in Sex Scenes." *Writer's Digest*, Volume 59, June 1979. pp. 22–24.

Heald, Tim. *A Life of Love: Barbara Cartland*. London: Sinclair-Stevenson. 1994.

Pearson, John. *Barbara Cartland: Crusader in Pink*. New York: Everest House. 1979.

Robyns, Gwen. *Barbara Cartland*. Boston, MA: G.K. Hall. 1984.

Severo, Richard. "Barbara Cartland, 98, Best-Selling Author Who Prized Old-Fashioned Romance, Dies." *New York Times*. May 22, 2000. p. B7. http://www.nytimes.com/2000/05/22/books/barbara-cartland-98-best-selling-author-who-prized-old-fashioned-romance-dies.html?pagewanted=all. Last visited January 2010.

Criticism and Readers' Guides

Brunt, Rosalind. "A Career in Love: The Romantic World of Barbara Cart-land." In *Fiction and Social Change*. Ed. Christopher Pawling. New York: St. Martin's Press. 1984. pp. 127–156.

Ryder, Mary Ellen. "Smoke and Mirrors: Event Patterns in the Discourse Struc-ture of a Romance Novel." *Journal of Pragmatics: An Interdisciplinary Jour-nal of Language Studies,* Volume 31, Issue 8, August 1999. pp. 1067–1080.

Sales, Roger. "The Loathsome Lord and the Disdainful Dame: Byron, Cart-land and the Regency Romance. In *Byronmania: Portraits of the Artist in Nineteenth and Twentieth Century Culture*. Ed. Frances Wilson and Alex Alec-Smith. Basingstoke, England: Macmillian Press. 1999. pp. 166–183.

Web Site

Barbara Cartland. http://www.barbaracartland.com/. Last visited December 2009. The official Barbara Cartland Web site including her extensive back list, biographical information, and links to additional Cartland Web sites.

Loretta Chase (1949–)

Historical Novels / Regency Novels

Biographical Sketch

Loretta Chase is the pseudonym used by Loretta Chekani. Loretta Chase's *Lord of Scoundrels* is routinely listed on romance Web sites and blogs as the "favorite" or "best" historical romance novel. Chase writes with humor but never forgets that she's writing about people who lived in a different time period. Her heroines are smart and brave, and never descend into the "too stupid to live" category. Her heroes are often of the nobility but are emotion-ally damaged. The settings, while usually during the Regency era or early Victorian era, may revolve around the *ton,* the aristocracy, but occasionally move to the exotic locales of Egypt or Albania.

Chase attended Clark University and graduated with a BA in English. Like most English majors, Chase aspired to writing the "great American novel"; but after a series of administrative assistant jobs, found the romance genre to be a good fit. Her novels are rigorously researched, which is the part of the writing process that Chase enjoys the most.

> *"You are the wickedest man who ever lived. And you eat small children for breakfast, their nannies tell them, if they are naughty."*
> *"But you are not in the least alarmed."*
> *"It is not breakfast time."*
>
> Loretta Chase
> *Lord of Scoundrels,* 1994

Major Works

Novels in Series

Fallen Women

Don't Tempt Me, 2009
Your Scandalous Ways, 2008
Not Quite a Lady, 2007

Carsington Brothers

Last Night's Scandal, 2010
Not Quite a Lady, 2007
Lord Perfect, 2006
Mr. Impossible, 2005
Miss Wonderful, 2004

Novels

The Last Hellion, 1998
Captives of the Night, 1994
Lord of Scoundrels, 1994
The Lion's Daughter, 1992
Sandalwood Princess, 1990

Knaves Wager, 1990
The Devil's Delilah, 1989
Viscount Vagabond, 1988
English Witch, 1988
Isabella, 1987

Other Writings

"Historical Romance—The Path I've Taken." In *North American Romance Writers.* Ed Kay Mussell and Johanna Tunon. London: Scarecrow Press. 1999. pp. 37–43.

Research Sources

Encyclopedias and Handbooks

"Loretta Chase." *Literature Resource Center.* (subscription database). 2008. http://galenet.galegroup.com/. Last visited July 2009.

Biographies and Interviews

Ana. "Chat with An Author and Giveaway: Loretta Chase." *The Book Smugglers.* June 19, 2009. http://thebooksmugglers.com/2009/06/chat-with-an-author-and-giveaway-loretta-chase.html. Last visited July 2009.
"At the Back Fence, Issue #217." *All About Romance.* March 6, 2006. http://www.likesbooks.com/217.html. Last visited April 2009.
Coleman, Sandy. "Writer's Corner for September 2006: Quick Q & A with Loretta Chase." *All About Romance.* September 2006. http://www.likesbooks.com/lorettachase2006.html. Last visited July 2009.
Holloway Scott, Susan. "Lord of Scoundrels Interview: Part One." *Word Wenches.* November 13, 2007. http://wordwenches.typepad.com/word_wenches/2007/11/lord-of-scoun-1.html. Last visited July 2009.

Holloway Scott, Susan. "Lord of Scoundrels Interview: Part Deux." *Word Wenches.* November 18, 2007. http://wordwenches.typepad.com/word_wenches/2007/11/lord-of-scoundr.html. Last visited July 2009.

Jorgenson, Jane. "Writer's Corner for February 2005: Loretta Chase Interview." *All About Romance.* February 2005. http://www.likesbooks.com/lorettachase.html. Last visited July 2009.

Web Sites

Loretta Chase. http://www.lorettachase.com/. Last visited December 2009. Official Web site of Loretta Chase; includes information about forthcoming books, biographical information, an FAQ, and a list of her upcoming appearances.

Loretta Chase In Other Words. http://lorettachase.blogspot.com/. Last visited December 2009. The official blog of Loretta Chase.

If You Like Loretta Chase

Loretta Chase writes Regency- and Victorian-era stories that are rigorously researched. Damaged emotionally, her heroes feel they cannot love, but her heroines are strong women who find that love is worth the risk.

You May Like

Mary Balogh

Mary Balogh writes character-driven Regency and Historical romances. Her books closely follow along the Jane Austen and Georgette Heyer style of historical novels focusing on marriage and accidentally finding love. She frequently features characters in several books, with minor characters in one novel becoming the hero or heroine in a subsequent novel.

Jo Beverley

Jo Beverley writes mostly series novels, such as her Malloren series, which focuses on the fates of the brothers and sisters of the Malloren family. Her titles cover the Georgian and Regency time periods and feature strong women and men who like strong women whether they know it or not. In 2000 her novel *Devilish* produced one of the most anticipated heroes of the 21st century in the Marquess of Rothgar.

Candice Hern

Candice Hern writes beautifully crafted Regency novels. Her detail about the time period, characters, and plots are authentic to the Regency era. Hern's multiple series allow the reader to revisit old characters in the new stories. If you can find Hern's early Signet Regencies in a used bookstore, you will have found some truly enjoyable Regency novels.

Lisa Kleypas

Known for strong romantic characters in a Regency setting, Kleypas novels feature characters that revolve around the *ton* but are not of the aristocracy itself. Her 1994 novel *Dreaming of You* is a wonderful example of Regency life built around the aristocracy.

Stephanie Laurens

Laurens's stories are character-driven and feature dominant male heroes, and heroines who are confident enough to stand up to them. While the stories take place during the Regency time period and can be emotional, they are not stuffy. Laurens's stories are all very sensual and can be humorous.

Mary Jo Putney

Mary Jo Putney writes an emotional story like no other. Her historical novels, especially the Fallen Angels, pull the reader into the time period through her richly layered characters. Putney has researched the Napoleonic wars extensively and effectively uses that as a backdrop.

Catherine Coulter (1942–)

Historical / Regency / Contemporary / Romantic Suspense / Category

Biographical Sketch

Catherine Coulter was born in Texas and graduated from the University of Texas. She continued her education with a master's degree in 19th century European history from Boston College. While her husband was in medical school, Coulter spent her nights reading romance novels and after a particularly bad one, stated that she could write a better one. Her husband challenged her to do just that, and her first Regency *Devilish* was released in 1978.

Coulter's works are bold and full of adventure. Her strong heroines are willing to fight for what they believe in. The heroes in a Coulter story come across as the alpha male, but with a softer side. Although they may have never seen love before, they want to believe in it.

Someone was watching her. She tugged on the black wig, flattening it against her ears, and quickly put on another coat of deep red lipstick, holding the mirror up so she could see behind her.

Catherine Coulter
The Cove, 1996

Major Works

Song Series

The Penwyth Curse, 2003
Rosehaven, 1996
Secret Song, 1991
Earth Song, 1990
Fire Song, 1985
Chandra, 1983 (reprinted as *Warrior's Song*)

Legacy Series

The Valentine Legacy, 1995
The Nightingale Legacy, 1994
The Wyndham Legacy, 1994
Devil's Daughter, 1985
Devil's Embrace, 1982

Night Series

Night Storm, 1990
Night Shadow, 1989
Night Fire, 1989

Magic Series

Moonspun Magic, 1988
Calypso Magic, 1988
Midsummer Magic, 1987

Star Series

Jade Star, 1986
Wild Star, 1986
Midnight Star, 1986
Evening Star, 1984

Regency Series

The Wild Baron, 1997
An Intimate Deception (reprinted as *The Deception*), 1983
An Honorable Offer (reprinted as *The Offer*), 1981
The Generous Earl (reprinted as *The Duke*), 1981
Lord Harry's Folly (reprinted as *Lord Harry*), 1980
Lord Deverill's Heir (reprinted as *The Heir*), 1980
The Rebel Bride, 1979
The Autumn Countess (reprinted as *The Countess*), 1978

Single Title Novels

Whiplash, 2010
KnockOut, 2009
TailSpin, 2008
Wizard's Daughter, 2008
Double Take, 2007
Born to be Wild, 2006
Point Blank, 2005
Lyon's Gate, 2005
Blowout, 2004
The Sherbrooke Twins, 2004
Blindside, 2003
Eleventh Hour, 2002
Pendragon, 2002
Hemlock Bay, 2001
Scottish Bride, 2001
Riptide, 2000
The Courtship, 2000

The Edge, 1999
Mad Jack, 1999
The Target, 1998
The Maze, 1997
The Wild Baron, 1997
The Cove, 1996
Lord of Falcon Ridge, 1995
Lord of Raven's Peak, 1994
Lord of Hawkfell Island, 1993
The Heiress Bride, 1993
The Hellion Bride, 1992
The Sherbrooke Bride, 1992
Beyond Eden, 1992
Season of the Sun, 1991
Impulse, 1990
False Pretenses, 1988

Category Novels

Afterglow, Silhouette Intimate Moment #190, 1987
The Aristocrat, Silhouette Special Edition #331, 1986
Aftershocks, Silhouette Intimate Moment #121, 1985

Research Sources

Encyclopedias and Handbooks

"Catherine Coulter." *Literature Resource Center.* (subscription database). 2008. http://galenet.galegroup.com/ Last visited July 2009.

Biographies and Interviews

Griffin, Glenn. "Maze Leaves Author Dazed." *Denver Post.* July 20, 1997.
Guiley, Rosemary. "Catherine Coulter." *Love Lines: A Romance Reader's Guide to Printed Pleasures.* New York: Facts on File Publications. 1983. pp. 206–207.
Saveri, Gabrielle. "Loving the Love Stuff." *People,* Volume 46, Issue 13, September 23, 1996. p. 34.
Sherwin, Elisabeth. "Coulter Dispenses Advice Like an Inspirational Speaker." *Printed Matter.* August 4, 1996. http://www.dcn.davis.ca.us/go/gizmo/coulter.html. Last visited July 2009.
"Some Time with Catherine Coulter." *All About Romance.* 1996. http://www.likesbooks.com/int7.html. Last visited July 2009.

Yamashita, Brianna. "From History to Mystery: A Genre-Jumper Explains: PW Talks with Catherine Coulter." *Publisher's Weekly,* Volume 250, Issue 26, June 30, 2003. p. 55.

Web Site

Catherine Coulter. http://www.catherinecoulter.com/. Last visited December 2009. The official Catherine Coulter Web site; includes biographical information, information on forthcoming books, and an FAQ.

Jennifer Crusie (1949–)

Contemporary Novels / Category Novels

Biographical Sketch

When you've had one of *those* days, pick up a Jennifer Crusie novel and laugh. Her novels feature sharp writing (okay, snark), wonderfully witty heroines with an equally witty support system, either family or friends, and heroes that may be flawed but understand the strength in the women they love. Crusie's earlier works are straight romance, while her more recent collaborations slide over to the chick-lit side of the romance genre.

Crusie received a bachelor's degree in art education from Bowling Green State University in 1971, and a master's degree in professional writing and women's literature from Wright State University. She began writing romance while she was working on her PhD dissertation on the differences in women's and men's narratives. As part of the dissertation process, Crusie planned to read 100 romance novels and 100 adventure novels. After falling in love with the romance genre she began her own romance novel and to this day her dissertation remains unfinished. Crusie is divorced and lives in Ohio; in 2009 her only daughter made Crusie a proud grandmother.

> *Once upon a time, Minerva Dobbs thought as she stood in the middle of a loud yuppie bar, the world was full of good men. She looked into the handsome face of the man she'd planned on as a date to her sister's wedding and thought, Those days are gone.*
>
> Jennifer Crusie
> *Bet Me,* 2007

Major Works

Novels in Series

Dempsey Family

Faking It, 2002
Welcome to Temptation, 2000

Novels

Maybe This Time, 2010
Bet Me, 2004
Fast Women, 2001
Crazy for You, 1999
Tell Me Lies, 1998

Harlequin Temptation

Charlie All Night, #570, 1996
What the Lady Wants, #544, 1995
Strange Bedpersons, #520, 1994
Getting Rid of Bradley, #480, 1994
Manhunting, #63, 1993

Other Category Novels

Trust Me on This, Loveswept #843, 1997
The Cinderella Deal, Loveswept #807, 1996
Anyone But You, Harlequin Love & Laughter #4, 1996
Sizzle, Silhouette Stolen Moments, 1994

Collaborations

With Bob Mayer

Wild Ride, 2010
Agnes and the Hitman, 2007
Don't Look Down, 2006

With Anne Stuart and Lani Diane Rich

Dogs and Goddesses, 2009
With Eileen Dreyer and Anne Stuart
The Unfortunate Miss Fortunes, 2007

Other Works

Nonfiction Books

*Flirting with Pride and Prejudice: Fresh Perspectives on the Original Chick Lit
    Masterpiece,* 2005
Totally Charmed: Demons, Whitelighters, and the Power of Three, 2005
Anne Rise: A Critical Companion, 1996

Essays

Crusie, Jennifer. "Jennifer Crusie." *The Writer,* Volume 117, Number 7, August
    2005, p. 62.

Crusie, Jennifer. "More from Jennifer Crusie." *The Writer Online.* June 7, 2004. http://www.writermag.com/wrt/default.aspx?c=a&id=1659. Last visited July 2009.

Crusie, Jennifer. "The Assassination of Cordelia Chase." *Five Seasons of Angel: Science Fiction and Fantasy Writers Discuss Their Favorite Vampire.* Ed. Glenn Yeffeth. Dallas: BenBella Books. 2004.

Crusie, Jennifer. "Dating Death." *Seven Seasons of Buffy: Science Fiction and Fantasy Writers Discuss Their Favorite Television Show.* Ed. Glenn Yeffeth. Dallas: BenBella Books. 2003.

Crusie, Jennifer. "Picture This: Collage as Prewriting and Inspiration." *Romance Writer's Report.* February 2003.

Crusie, Jennifer. "Emotionally Speaking: Romance Fiction in the Twenty-First Century." *Writer's Market.* 2003.

Crusie, Jennifer. "Don't Do This At Home: The Four Biggest Mistakes in Contest Entries." *Romance Writer's Report.* October 2001.

Crusie, Jennifer. "Comedy Workshop." *How To Write Funny: Add Humor to Every Kind of Writing.* Ed. John B. Kachuba. Cincinnati, OH: Writer's Digest Books, 2001.

Crusie, Jennifer. "Why I Sometimes Think About Not Writing Romance Fiction/Why I'll Write Romance Fiction Until They Pry My Cold Dead Fingers from Around My Keyboard." In *North American Romance Writers.* Ed. Kay Mussell and Johanna Tunon. London: Scarecrow Press. 1999. pp. 221–226.

Crusie Jennifer. "Romantic Comedy, the No-Calorie Godiva." *Springs Literary Supplement.* Volume 16, Number 2, February 1998, p. 22.

Smith, Jennifer. "This is Not Your Mother's Cinderella: The Romance Novel as Feminist Fairy Tale." *Romantic Conventions.* Ed. Anne Kaler and Rosemary Johnson-Kurek. Bowling Green: Bowling Green Popular Press. 1998.

Smith, Jennifer. "The Romantic Suspense Mystery." *Mystery and Suspense Writers: The Literature of Crime, Detection, and Espionage.* New York: Scribner's. 1998.

Smith, Jennifer. "Romancing Reality: The Power of Romance Fiction to Reinforce and Re-Vision the Real." *Paradoxa: Studies in World Literary Genres,* Numbers 1–2, 1997. pp. 81–93.

Research Sources

Encyclopedias and Handbooks

Charles, John and Hamilton-Selway, Joanne. "Jennifer Crusie." In *Romance Today: An A-To-Z Guide to Contemporary American Romance Writers.* Ed. John Charles and Shelley Mosley. Westport, CT: Greenwood. 2007. pp. 69–73.

"Jennifer Smith." *Literature Resource Center.* (subscription database). 2008. http://galenet.galegroup.com/. Last visited June 2009.

Biographies and Interviews

"Author Jennifer Crusie Discusses Her Influences." *RT Book Reviews Magazine.* March 9, 2010. http://vimeo.com/10036471. Last visited March 2010.

Block, Allison. "A Sure Bet: Jennifer Crusie's Rollicking Romance Hits the Jackpot." *Book Page Web site.* http://www.bookpage.com/0402bp/jennifer_crusie.html. Last visited July 2009.

Bloom, Taylor. "Spotlight Article: Interview with Jennifer Crusie." *Romance Writers of America, Greater Vancouver Chapter.* July 2007. http://www.rwagvc.com/newsletter/jul2007.html. Last visited July 2009.

Hall, Melissa Mia. "PW Talks with Jennifer Crusie." *Publisher's Weekly,* Volume 249, Issue 30, July 29, 2002. p. 52.

Jorgenson, Jane. "Writer's Corner: Jennifer Crusie." *All About Romance.* October 2004. http://www.likesbooks.com/crusie.html. Last visited July 2009.

"Literaturschock Interview Mit Jennifer Crusie." *Literaturschock.* 2002. http://www.literaturschock.de/autorengefluester/000005. Last visited July 2009.

Maryles, Daisy. "She Said, He Said: Sparks Fly When a Top Romance Novelist Meets a Thriving Thriller Writer." *Publisher's Weekly,* Volume 253, Issue 10, March 6, 2006. p. 32.

Sova, Cathy. "Catching Up with Jennifer Crusie." *The Romance Reader.* August 19, 2002. http://www.theromancereader.com/crusie.html. Last visited July 2009.

Other Resources

Weber, Bruce. "Romance Novelists: Profits Without Honor." *New York Times.* August 3, 1999. p. E1. http://www.nytimes.com/1999/08/03/books/arts-in-america-romance-novelists-profits-without-honor.html?pagewanted=1. Last visited January 2010.

Web Sites

Jenny Crusie. http://www.jennycrusie.com/. Last visited December 2009. The official Jennifer Crusie Web site; includes complete publication list, biographical information, information for aspiring writers, and a blog.

Argh Ink. http://www.arghink.com/. Last visited December 2009. Crusie's official blog site.

The Cherry Forums. http://www.cherryforums.com/. Last visited December 2009. An open forum to discuss the reading and writing of romance novels.

If You Like Jennifer Crusie

Crusie's stories revolve around friendships, family, and love in a very entertainingly (snarky) way, with imperfect heroines who are often required to solve problems that they didn't make and heroes who are smart, strong, and willing to work for love.

You May Like

Cathie Linz

Cathie Linz writes fun, contemporary stories, that feature often unconventional heroines and heroes smart enough to love them. There are no overly emotional struggles or serial killers to be found in a Linz story.

Kasey Michaels

Kasey Michaels writers laugh-out-loud funny historical and contemporary romances. Her contemporary stories feature heroines who can see possibilities beyond their current lives, while her heroes are often outrageous, as in the Maggie Kelly series.

Susan Elizabeth Phillips

Susan Elizabeth Phillips writes stories with often imperfect, struggling heroines and strong males who know what they want and work hard to get it. Humor and strong characters are always key elements in any Philips novel.

Janet Dailey (1944–)

Contemporary / Category / Historical

Biographical Sketch

At one time, Janet Dailey was one of the most popular writers in the romance genre. Dailey married her husband after working with him in the construction industry in Nebraska. After complaining to her husband that should write a better romance novel than what she was reading, Bill challenged her to do it. When Dailey's first book was accepted by Harlequin in 1974, she became Harlequin's first American author. In the 1980s, Dailey and her husband moved to Branson, Missouri, where she still resides.

Dailey is known for having pushed the envelope on sex scenes as the romance novel industry was becoming more popular. While traveling around the country by RV in the 1970s and 80s, Dailey wrote a novel for each state; those novels became her Americana Series.

In 1997 Dailey was accused of plagiarizing several of Nora Roberts's works in the novels *Aspen Gold, Notorious,* and another novel that was never released. The lawsuit was settled out of court in 1998 with Dailey paying Roberts a settlement.

"In case you don't know, there are two kinds of love. The most popular is the instant, fire-and-flames kind, with rockets going off and bells ringing. But there's another kind of love, one that sneaks up on you. One day you turn around and there it is–strong and deep and true."

Janet Dailey
Illusions, 1997

Major Works

Novels in Series

Calder Saga

Calder Storm, volume 10, 2006
Lone Calder Sky, volume 9, 2005
Calder Promise, volume 8, 2004
Shifting Calder Wind, volume 7, 2003
Green Calder Grass, volume 6, 2002

Calder Pride, volume 5, 1999
Calder Born, Calder Bred, volume 4, 1983
Stands a Calder Man, volume 2, 1983
This Calder Sky, volume 3, 1981
This Calder Range, volume 1, 1981

Single Title Novels

Scrooge Wore Spurs, 2002
A Capital Holiday, 2001
Illusions, 1997
Notroious, 1996
Legacies, 1995
The Proud and the Free, 1994
Tangled Vines, 1992
Aspen Gold, 1991
Masquerade, 1990
Rivals, 1989

Heiress, 1987
The Great Alone, 1986
The Glory Game, 1985
The Pride of Hannah Wade, 1985
Silver Wings, Santiago Blue, 1984
Night Way, 1981
Ride the Thunder, 1980
The Rogue, 1980
Touch the Wind, 1979

Harlequin Presents

That Carolina Summer, #488, 1982
With a Little Luck, #482, 1982
Northern Magic, #475, 1982
Dakota Dreaming, #445, 1981
The Traveling Kind, #427, 1981
A Tradition of Pride, #421, 1981
Wild and Wonderful, #416, 1981
One of the Boys, #399, 1980
Heart of Stone, #391, 1980
Difficult Decision, #386, 1980
Enemy in Camp, #373, 1980
Southern Nights, #369, 1980

Lord of the High Lonesome, #363, 1980
The Mating Season, #356, 1980
The Thawing of Mara, #349, 1980
Bed of Grass, #343, 1980
That Boston Man, #338, 1980
Kona Winds, #332, 1980
A Land Called Deseret, #326, 1979
Sentimental Journey, #319, 1979
For Mike's Sake, #313, 1979
Sweet Promise, #308, 1979
Low Country Liar, #302, 1979

Strange Bedfellow, #296, 1979
Tidewater Lover, #292, 1979
The Bride of the Delta Queen, #284, 1979
Summer Mahogany, #279, 1979
Six White Horses, #275, 1979
Green Mountain Man, #272, 1979
For Bitter or Worse, #267, 1979
The Matchmakers, #264, 1978
Giant of Mesabi, #259, 1978
Beware of the Stranger, #256, 1978
The Master Fiddler, #252, 1978
Something Extra, #248, 1978
Big Sky Country, #244, 1978
Sonora Sundown, #239, 1978
To Tell the Truth, #236, 1978
Reiley's Woman, #231, 1978
Darling Jenny, #227, 1978

The Indy Man, #223, 1978
The Ivory Cane, #219, 1978
The Widow and the Wastrel, #211, 1977
A Lyon's Share, #208, 1977
Bluegrass King, #203, 1977
Show Me, #200, 1977
Fiesta San Antonio, #192, 1977
Valley of the Vapours, #183, 1977
Night of the Coltillion, #180, 1977
Dangerous Masquerade, #171, 1977
After the Storm, #167, 1976
The Homeplace, #159, 1976
Land of Enchantment, #151, 1976
Fire and Ice, #147, 1976
Savage Land, #139, 1976
Boss Man from Ogallala, #131, 1976
No Quarter Asked, #124, 1976

Silhouette Romance

Separate Cabins, #213, 1983
Mistletoe and Holly, #195, 1982
The Second Time, #177, 1982
Wildcatter's Woman, #153, 1982
For the Love of God, #118, 1981
The Lancaster Men, #106, 1981
Hostage Bride, #82, 1981

Silhouette Special Edition

Leftover Love, #150, 1984
The Best Way, #132, 1983
Foxfire Light, #36, 1982
Terms of Surrender, #1, 1982

Other Works

The Janet Dailey Companion: A Comprehensive Guide to Her Life and Her Novels, 1996.

Research Sources

Encyclopedias and Handbooks

"Janet Dailey." *Literature Resource Center.* (subscription database). (2009). http://galenet.galegroup.com./ Last visited July 2009.

Whitehead, Frances. "Janet Dailey." In *Twentieth-Century Romance and Historical Writers*. Ed. Aruna Vasudevan. 3rd ed. London: St. James Press. 1990. pp. 161–163.

Biographies and Interviews

Falk, Kathryn. "Janet Dailey." *Love's Leading Ladies*. New York: Pinnacle Books. 1982. pp. 77–83.

Guiley, Rosemary. "Janet Dailey." *Love Lines: A Romance Reader's Guide to Printed Pleasures*. New York: Facts on File Publications. 1983. pp. 209–210.

Hall, Wesley. "Interview with Janet Dailey." *OzarksWatch,* Volume 8, Issue 3, 1995. http://thelibrary.springfield.missouri.org/lochist/periodicals/ozarks watch/ow803e.htm. Last visited July 2009.

Keeney, Carole. "Dailey's Life Unfolds Like Her Books End—Happily Ever After." *Houston Chronicle.* July 6, 1986. http://www.chron.com/CDA/ar chives/archive.mpl?id=1986_250454. Last visited July 2009.

Mooradian, Jill Bloom. "Who Writes the Books of Love." *Boston Globe.* December 6, 1981.

Mussell, Kay. "Paradoxa Interview with Janet Dailey." *Paradoxa: Studies in World Literary Genres,* Volume 3, Issues 1–2, 1997. pp. 214–218.

Thompson, Jim. "It's Not What You Know…It's What You Learn." *Writer's Digest,* Volume 75, Issue 1, January 1996. p. 6.

Criticism and Readers' Guides

Chappel, Deborah Kay. *American Romances: Narratives of Culture and Identity*. PhD Dissertation. Duke University. 1991.

McClain, Larry. "Women's Studies, Cultural Studies: Teaching Literature in the Midwest. *Transformations*, Volume 7, Issue 1, March 31, 1996. pp. 15–28.

Other Resources

Bolotin, Susan. "Janet Dailey." *New York Time Book Review.* August 16, 1981. p. 26.

Fisher, Lawrence M. "Making a Difference: Mondavi Pours New Wines and Adds a Whiff of Romance." *New York Times,* August 30, 1992. p. A10. http:// www.nytimes.com/1992/08/30/business/making-a-difference-mondavi- pours-new-wines-and-adds-a-whiff-of-romance.html?pagewanted=1. Last visited January 2010.

"Laurie's News & Views." *All About Romance,* Issue 28. June 28, 1997. http:// www.likesbooks.com/28.html. Last visited July 2009.

"Laurie's News & Views." *All About Romance,* Issue 30. July 30, 1997. http:// www.likesbooks.com/30.html. Last visited July 2009.

Parisi, Joseph. "Janet Dailey: Readers Love Her, Critics Ignore Her." *Book World.* June 12, 1983. pp. 1, 31.

Patrick, Diane. "Dailey, Roberts Settle Copyright Infringement Suite." *Publisher's Weekly,* Volume 245, Issue 18, May 4, 1998. p. 18.

Peyser, Marc and Chang, Yahlin. "The Queen of Hearts Gives Up Her Throne." *Newsweek,* Volume 130, Issue 6, August 11, 1997. pp. 74–76.

Streitfeld, David. "Stolen Kisses!: Romance Writer Lifts Another's Bodice of Work." *Washington Post.* July 30, 1997. p. C1.

Web Site

Janet Dailey. http://www.janetdailey.com/. Last visited December 2009. The official Janet Dailey Web site; includes a backlist of her novels, an FAQ, and brief updates on Dailey's current life.

Jude Deveraux (1947–)

Historical / Medieval / Romantic Suspense / Paranormal

Biographical Sketch

Jude Deveraux is the pseudonym used by Jude Gilliam White, who grew up in Kentucky and received a bachelor's degree from Murray State University. After graduation, Deveraux worked as a school teacher in Santa Fe, New Mexico. She has been married twice and divorced twice.

Deveraux writes sweeping historical stories set in turbulent times, such as the French Revolution, the American Revolution, and the Tudor era. Her stories feature strong women who are more than just decorations, who are intelligent and hard working. The heroes are alpha males but recognize the strength in the women they love. Usually there is some type of misunderstanding between the hero and the heroine. Deveraux's time travel novel *Knight in Shining Armor* is often listed as a favorite among romance readers.

> *Suddenly he felt a swift wave of jealousy. He'd never seen this woman who sat so calmly before these men and made decisions that affected their lives. They knew a side of her that he'd never even guessed at.*
>
> Jude Deveraux
> *Highland Velvet,* 1982

Major Works

Novels

Montgomery Family

Someone to Love, 2007
Always, 2004
Forever and Always, 2003

Forever: A Novel of Good and Evil, Love and Hope, 2002
High Tide, 1999

The Heiress, 1996
Eternity, 1992
The Duchess, 1991
A Knight in Shining Armor, 1989
Wishes, 1989
The Awakening, 1988
The Maiden, 1988
The Princess, 1987

The Raider, 1987
The Temptress, 1986
Velvet Angel, 1983
Velvet Song, 1983
Highland Velvet, 1982
The Velvet Promise, 1980
The Black Lyon, 1980

Taggart Family

Holly, 2003
Sweet Liar, 1992
Twin of Ice, 1985
Twin of Fire, 1985

James River

River Lady, 1985
Lost Lady, 1985
Counterfeit Lady, 1984
Sweetbriar, 1983

Peregrine Family

The Conquest, 1991
The Taming, 1989

Single Title Novels

Scarlet Nights, 2010
Days of Gold, 2009
Lavender Morning, 2009
Return to Summerhouse, 2008
Secrets, 2008
Someone to Love, 2007
Carolina Isle, 2006
First Impressions, 2005
Always, 2004
Wild Orchids, 2003

The Mulberry Tree, 2002
The Summerhouse, 2001
Temptation, 2000
High Tide, 1999
The Blessing, 1999
An Angel for Emily, 1998
Legend, 1996
Remembrance, 1994
The Conquest, 1991
Enchanted Land, 1978

Research Sources

Encyclopedias and Handbooks

"Jude Deveraux." *Literature Resource Center.* (subscription database). 2009. http://galenet.galegroup.com/. Last visited July 2009.

Rhodes, Judith. "Jude Deveraux." In *Twentieth-Century Romance and Historical Writers.* Ed. Aruna Vasudevan. 3rd ed. London: St. James Press. 1990. pp. 182–184.

Biographies and Interviews

Falk, Kathryn. "Jude Deveraux." *Love's Leading Ladies.* New York: Pinnacle Books. 1982. pp. 91–95.
Guiley, Rosemary. "Jude Deveraux." *Love Lines: A Romance Reader's Guide to Printed Pleasures.* New York: Facts on File Publications. 1983. pp. 211–212.
"Jude Deveraux: Author Revealed." *Simon and Schuster.* http://authors.simo nandschuster.com/Jude-Deveraux/1445134/author_revealed. Last visited July 2009.
Wehr, Isolde. "Interview with Jude Deveraux." *The Romantic Bookcorner.* 2001. http://www.die-buecherecke.de/e_index.htm. Last visited July 2009.

Criticism and Readers' Guides

Breslin, Carol Ann. "Medieval Magic and Witchcraft in the Popular Romance Novel." In *Romantic Conventions.* Ed. Anne K. Kaler and Rosemary E. Johnson-Kurek. Bowling Green, OH: Popular. 1999. pp. 75–85.
Chappel, Deborah Kay. *American Romances: Narratives of Culture and Identity.* PhD Dissertation. Duke University. 1991.

Web Site

Jude Deveraux does not have an official Web site.

Eileen Dreyer / Kathleen Korbel

Category / Contemporary / Romantic Suspense

Biographical Sketch

Eileen Dreyer writes mystery and suspense novels under her own name and romance novels under the name of Kathleen Korbel. Dreyer's novel *A Rose for Maggie* is listed as a "favorite" category novel on many lists and blogs. Both the romance and mystery novels contain characters that face extraordinary challenges, such as posttraumatic stress disorder or a child with Down syndrome, in very human ways. However, there are no superheroes in her stories, just men and women trying to live life in the best way they can.

Dreyer received her RN degree in 1972 and continued her education with a BS in 1982. She has used her experience as a trauma nurse in two of St. Louis's busiest trauma centers and her training in forensic nursing as inspiration for her works. Recently, Dreyer attended "Swat Camp" with her local police department to obtain firsthand research for her mystery novels. Dreyer continues to live in Missouri with her husband and children and Dreyer is a member of the Romance Writers of America Hall of Fame.

> *But that summer was even worse. A cicada population of Biblical proportions had awakened from two separate periods of dormancy to drive every person in the bi-state region to violence. Breeding and eating at a ferocious rate in their hurry to mate and die, the insects whined out a satanic symphony of grinding dissonance that could incite a saint to suicide.*

Eileen Dreyer
With a Vengeance, 2003

Major Works

Novels

Novels Written as Eileen Dreyer

Barely a Lady, 2010
Sinners and Saints, 2005
Head Games, 2004
With a Vengeance, 2003
Brain Dead, 1997
Bad Medicine, 1995
Nothing Personal, 1994
If Looks Could Kill, 1992
A Man to Die For, 1991

Silhouette Intimate Moments Titles Written as Kathleen Korbel

Some Men's Dreams, #1237, 2003
A Soldier's Heart, #602, 1995
Simple Gifts, #571, 1994
Walk on the Wild Side, #457, 1992
Jake's Way, #413, 1992
A Rose for Maggie, #396, 1991

Lightning Strikes, #351, 1990
The Ice Cream Man, #309, 1989
Perchance to Dream, #276, 1989
Edge of the World, #222, 1988
Worth Any Risk, #191, 1987
A Stranger's Smile, #163, 1986

Silhouette Desire Titles Written as Kathleen Korbel

Sail Away, #1254, 1998
Don't Fence Me In, #1015, 1996
Isn't It Romantic?, #703, 1992
A Fine Madness, #668, 1991

Hotshot, #582, 1990
The Princess and the Pea, #455, 1988
A Prince of a Guy, #389, 1987
Playing the Game, #286, 1986

Silhouette Nocturne Titles Written as Kathleen Korbel

Deadly Redemption, #47, 2008
Dark Seduction, #34, 2008
Dangerous Temptation, #2, 2007

Collaborations

With Jennifer Crusie and Anne Stuart

The Unfortunate Ms. Fortunes, 2007

Other Works

Essays

Dreyer, Eileen. "And I Still Write Romance." In *North American Romance Writers.* Ed. Kay Mussell and Johanna Tunon. London: Scarecrow Press. 1999. pp. 73–78.

Dreyer, Eileen. "It was Much Easier When I Just Had to Shoot People." *Risky Regencies.* March 25, 2009. http://riskyregencies.blogspot.com/2009/03/it-was-much-easier-when-i-just-had-to.html. Last visited July 2009.

Research Sources

Encyclopedias and Handbooks

Charles, John. "Eileen Dreyer." In *Romance Today: An A-To-Z Guide to Contemporary American Romance Writers.* Ed. John Charles and Shelley Mosley. Westport, CT: Greenwood. 2007. pp. 81–85.

"Eileen Dreyer." *Literature Resource Center.* (subscription database). 2008. http://galenet.galegroup.com/. Last visited June 2009.

Biographies and Interviews

"Author Interview: Eileen Dreyer." *HarperCollins.* http://www.harpercollins.com/author/authorExtra.aspx?authorID=2639&displayType=interview. Last visited July 2009.

Bexte, Martina. "Eileen Dreyer's Back with A Vengeance." *BookLoons.* March 2004. http://www.bookloons.com/cgi-bin/Columns.asp?type=Interview&name=Eileen%20Dreyer. Last visited July 2009.

Hall, Melissa Mia. "PW Talks with Eileen Dreyer: Tough Lessons in Nursing." *Publisher's Weekly,* Volume 250, Issue 9, March 3, 2003. p. 54.

"Please Welcome our March Featured Author, Eileen Dreyer." *New Mystery Reader Magazine.* http://www.newmysteryreader.com/eileen_dreyer.htm. Last visited July 2009.

Web Site

Eileen Dreyer. http://www.eileendreyer.com/. Last visited December 2009. The official Web site of Eileen Dreyer; includes a book list, photos of the author; links to appearances, and links to her favorite research Web sites.

Daphne du Maurier (1907–1989)

Romantic Suspense / Historical

Biographical Sketch

Daphne du Maurier created one of the most compelling romantic suspense novels of all time in *Rebecca.* Originally, du Maurier's novels were compared to the Gothic stories of the Brontë sisters, but with each additional novel, du Maurier's skill for creating tight, suspenseful plots grew. Her novel *Rebecca* is one of her most famous works and demonstrates her strong characterization skills. In 1940, Alfred Hitchcock directed Joan Fontaine and Laurence Olivier in the classic film version of *Rebecca.* In addition to her novels, du Maurier also wrote many plays, nonfiction works, and short stories including the short story *The Birds,* which Hitchcock also adapted for the big screen.

Du Maurier was born in London, England, to conservative parents who worked in the theater. She struggled with her sexual identity for most of her life, and did have affairs with women. In 1932, she married Major Frederick Arthur Browning and followed her husband around the world for the next several years. The couple had three children. In 1943, du Maurier leased a Cornwall mansion, and lived in Cornwall for the rest of her life. After the war Major Browning was knighted, giving du Maurier the title Lady Browning. In 1969, du Maurier was made a Dame of the British Empire in honor of her literary achievements. Du Maurier died in Cornwall in 1989.

> *Last night I dreamt I went to Manderley again. It seemed to me I stood by the iron gate leading to the drive, and for a while I could not enter for the way was barred to me.*
>
> Daphne du Maurier
> *Rebecca,* 1938

Major Works

Novels

Rule Britannia, 1972
The House on the Strand, 1969
The Flight of the Falcon, 1965
The Glass-Blowers, 1963
The Infernal World of Branwell Brontë,
    1960
The Scapegoat, 1957
Mary Anne: A Novel, 1954
My Cousin Rachel, 1951
The Parasites, 1949

The King's General, 1946
Hungry Hill, 1943
Frenchman's Creek, 1941
Come Wind, Come Weather, 1940
Rebecca, 1938
Jamaica Inn, 1936
The Progress of Julius, 1933
I'll Never Be Young Again, 1932
The Loving Spirit, 1931

Plays

September Tide: A Play in Three Acts, 1948
The Years Between: A Play in Two Acts, 1945

Other Works

Growing Pains: The Shaping of a Writer, 1977
The Winding Stair: Francis Bacon, His Rise and Fall, 1976
Golden Lads: Anthony Bacon, Francis and Their Friends, 1975
Vanishing Cornwall, 1967
Happy Christmas, 1940
The du Mauriers, 1937
Gerald: A Portrait, 1934

Movies Based on the Novels of Daphne du Maurier

Hamer, Robert, director. *The Scapegoat,* motion picture. August 6, 1959. Internet Movie Database, http://www.imdb.com/title/tt0053247/. Last visited September 2009.

Hitchcock, Alfred, director. *Rebecca,* motion picture. April 12, 1940. Internet Movie Database, http://www.imdb.com/title/tt0032976/. Last visited September 2009.

Koster, Henry, director. *My Cousin Rachel,* motion picture. December 24, 1954. Internet Movie Database, http://www.imdb.com/title/tt0044937/. Last visited September 2009.

Leisen, Mitchell, director. *Frenchman's Creek,* motion picture. September 20, 1944. Internet Movie Database, http://www.imdb.com/title/tt0036840/. Last visited September 2009.

Research Sources

For additional research sources please consult your library catalog, the MLA Bibliography, or your librarian for assistance. Below is a sample of the resources available.

Encyclopedias and Handbooks

"Daphne du Maurier." *Literature Resource Center.* (subscription database). 2003. http://galenet.galegroup.com/. Last visited June 2009.

Harris, June. "Daphne du Maurier: Overview." In *Contemporary Popular Writers.* Ed. Dave Mote. Detroit, MI: St. James Press. 1997.

Templeton, Wayne. "Daphne du Maurier." *Dictionary of Literary Biography: British Novelists Between the Wars.* Volume 191. Detroit, MI: Gale Research. 1998. pp. 85–94.

Biographies and Interviews

Auerbach, Nina. *Daphne du Maurier: Haunted Heiress.* Philadelphia, PA: University of Pennsylvania Press. 2000.

Cook, Judith. *Daphne: A Portrait of Daphne du Maurier.* London: Bantam Publishers. 1991.

Forster, Margaret. *Daphne du Maurier: The Secret Life of the Renowned Storyteller.* New York: Doubleday Publisher. 1993.

Shallcross, Martyn. *The Private World of Daphne du Maurier.* New York: St. Martin's Press. 1992.

Criticism and Readers' Guides

Blackford, Holly. "Haunted Housekeeping: Fatal Attractions of Servant and Mistress in Twentieth-Century Female Gothic Literature." *LIT: Literature, Interpretation, Theory,* Volume 16, Issue 2, 2005. pp. 233–261.

Horner, Avril. *Daphne du Maurier: Writing, Identity, and the Gothic Imagination.* New York: St. Martin's Press. 1998.

Taylor, Helen. The Daphne du Maurier Companion. London: Virago Press. 2007.

Web Site

Daphne du Maurier. http://www.dumaurier.org/. Last visited December 2009. A fan Web site devoted to du Maurier, including a member's forum, links to literary resources, and biographical information.

Kathleen Eagle (1947–)

Contemporary / Historical / Category

Biographical Sketch

Kathleen Eagle grew up as an "Air Force brat," traveling all over the country. She holds a BA in English Literature from Mount Holyoke College and an MS from Northern State University. She became an English teacher in North Dakota and eventually served as president of the North Dakota Council of Teachers of English. Besides writing novels, Eagle also reviewed books for the *Minneapolis Star Tribune*. Her husband is a member of the Lakota Sioux and also a school teacher. Eagle has three grown children, and she and her husband live in Minnesota.

Eagle's books frequently feature Native American characters in a very realistic light; she does not shy away from the issues facing Native Americans in contemporary culture. Eagle has received the Lifetime Achievement Award from *Romantic Times Magazine*.

Autumn was a season of majesty in Wyoming.

The Grand Teton Mountains wore the coming of winter in fierce glory, like a legion of emperors. Shy quaking aspens donned yellow for the occasion, dressing up the red road cuts, the black-green stands of pine, and the striations of granite and snow touching the heavens.

Kathleen Eagle
The Last Good Man, 2000

Major Works

Novels

Mystic Horseman, 2008
Ride a Painted Pony, 2006
A View of the River, 2005
Night Falls Like Silk, 2003
Once Upon a Wedding, 2002
You Never Can Tell, 2001
The Last Good Man, 2000

What the Heart Knows, 1999
The Last True Cowboy, 1998
The Night Remembers, 1997
Sunrise Song, 1996
Reason to Believe, 1995
Fire and Rain, 1994
This Time Forever, 1992

Silhouette Special Editions

Once a Father, #2066, 2010
In Care of Sam Beaudry, #1969, 2009
'Til There Was You, #576, 1990
Candles in the Night, #437, 1988
Something Worth Keeping, #359, 1987

Carved in Stone, #396, 1987
Broomstick Cowboy, #848, 1993
Georgia Nights, #304, 1986
Someday Soon, #204, 1984

Silhouette Intimate Moments

Defender, #589, 1994
Diamond Willow, #480, 1993
Black Tree Moon, #451, 1992
To Each His Own, #428, 1992
Bad Moon Rising, #412, 1991
Paintbox Morning, #284, 1989
But That Was Yesterday, #257, 1988
For Old Times' Sake, #148, 1986

Harlequin Historical

Heaven and Earth, #50, 1990
Medicine Woman, #30, 1989
Private Treaty, #2, 1988

Other Works

"Forget the Fluff." In *North American Romance Writers.* Ed. Kay Mussell
   and Johanna Tunon. London: Scarecrow Press. 1999. pp. 79–85.
"A Quickie with Kathleen Eagle on "Indian" P.C." *All About Romance.* No-
   vember 19, 1997. http://www.likesbooks.com/indian2.html. Last visited
   July 2009.
"A Quickie from Kathleen Eagle about Fiction versus Real Life." *All About
   Romance.* August 1997. http://www.likesbooks.com/quickie3.html. Last
   visited July 2009.

Research Sources

Encyclopedias and Handbooks

"Kathleen Eagle." *Literature Resource Center.* (subscription database). 2008.
   http://galenet.galegroup.com/. Last visited July 2009.

Biographies and Interviews

"Kathleen Eagle Armchair Interview." *Armchair Interviews: Author Interviews.*
   April 26, 2005. http://www.armchairinterviews.com/past-guests/audio/.
   Last visited July 2009.
"RBL Presents!: Kathleen Eagle." *RBL Romantica.* http://www.geocities.
   com/rblinterviews/eagleinterview.html. Last visited July 2009.

"Write Byte: An Author Who Reviews." *All About Romance.* September 17, 1997. http://www.likesbooks.com/review.html. Last visited July 2009.

Web Site

Kathleen Eagle. http://www.kathleeneagle.com/. Last visited December 2009. Kathleen Eagle's official Web site; includes biographical information, photos of the author, a news section, and a list of her books.

Christine Feehan

Contemporary / Paranormal

Biographical Sketch

Christine Feehan always wrote, especially when she was supposed to be doing schoolwork and later as the mother of eleven children. While raising her children, Feehan, a third-degree black belt, taught martial arts. Feehan shared a vampire story with friends, and they insisted she send her work to a publisher. The resulting novel, *Dark Prince,* was published in 1999. In 2007, Feehan published *Dark Hunger,* part of her Dark series, as a Manga comic book.

Feehan writes stories in series, using a different paranormal element for each such as vampires and vampire hunters in the Dark series, psychic abilities in the Leopard series, and magic in the Drake Sister books. Feehan uses a variety of locations and her stories are steamy with powerful, demanding heroes and intelligent heroines who are strong enough to be the equal of her heroes.

> *He refused to understand that was who she was—what she was. In rejecting her legacy, he rejected her. And she needed a man who would help her. Who would understand how difficult it was for her to face her future.*
>
> Christine Feehan
> *Hidden Currents,* 2009

Major Works

Novels in Series

The Dark Series

Dark Peril, 2010	*Dark Secret,* 2005
Dark Slayer, 2009	*Dark Destiny,* 2004
Dark Curse, 2008	*Dark Melody,* 2003
Dark Possession, 2007	*Dark Symphony,* 2003
Dark Hunger, 2007	*Dark Guardian,* 2002
Dark Celebration, 2006	*Dark Legend,* 2002
Dark Demon, 2006	*Dark Fire,* 2001

Dark Challenge, 2000
Dark Magic, 2000
Dark Gold, 2000

Dark Desire, 1999
Dark Prince, 1999

The Leopard Series

Wild Fire, 2010
Burning Wild, 2009
Fever, 2006
Wild Rain, 2004

Ghostwalkers

Street Game, 2009
Murder Game, 2008
Predatory Game, 2008
Deadly Game, 2007
Conspiracy Game, 2006
Night Game, 2005
Mind Game, 2004
Shadow Game, 2003

Sisters of the Heart

Water Bound, 2010

Drake Sisters

Hidden Currents, 2009
Turbulent Sea, 2008
Safe Harbor, 2007
Dangerous Tides, 2006
Magic in the Wind, 2005
Oceans of Fire, 2005
The Twilight Before Christmas, 2003

Novels

Lair of the Lion, 2002
The Scarletti Curse, 2001

Collaborations

With Melanie George

A Very Gothic Christmas, 2001

Research Sources

Encyclopedias and Handbooks

"Christine Feehan." *Literature Resource Center.* (subscription database.)
    2009. http://galenet.galegroup.com/. Last visited December 2009.

Biographies and Interviews

Jaymi. "Christine Feehan." *Fallen Angel Reviews.* 2004. http://fallenange lreviews.com/Interviews/2004/Feb04-Jaymi-ChristineFeehan.htm. Last visited December 2009.

Rock, Bonnie. "Writerspace Interview with Christine Feehan." *Writespace.* April 2003. http://www.writerspace.com/interviews/feehan0403.html. Last visited December 2009.

Weiss, Angela "Interview with Christine Feehan." *Die Romantische Bucherecke.* http://www.die-buecherecke.de/feehan2.htm. Last visited December 2009.

White, Claire E. "A Conversation with Christine Feehan." *Writers Write.* March 2002. http://www.writerswrite.com/journal/mar02/feehan.htm. Last visited December 2009.

Criticism and Readers' Guides

Lee, Linda J. "Guilty Pleasures: Reading Romance Novels as Reworked Fairy Tales." *Marvels & Tales: Journal of Fairy Tale Studies,* Volume 22, Issue 1, 2008. pp. 52–66.

Schell, Heather. "The Big Bad Wolf: Masculinity and Genetics in Popular Culture." *Literature and Medicine,* Volume 26, Issue 1, Spring 2007. pp. 109–125.

Web Site

Christine Feehan. http://www.christinefeehan.com/index.php. Last visited December 2009. The official webpage of Christine Feehan; includes biographical information, a backlist of titles with excerpts, a FAQ, and extensive research pages for her various series.

Lori Foster / L. L. Foster (1958–)

Contemporary / Category / Paranormal

Biographical Sketch

Lori Foster writes sexy romance novels under her own name and uses the pseudonym L. L. Foster to write urban fantasy novels. A stay-at home-mom, Foster began writing romance novels mostly for her own enjoyment for five years. After completing about ten different stories, and receiving many rejection letters, she sold her first story, *Impetuous,* in 1996. Several of those early works have subsequently been published, such as *Say Yes* and *Sex Appeal.* Foster, married after high school, has three grown sons, and is a grandmother.

Foster's stories are much more sexy than many other novels, and she was the first author published in the short-lived Harlequin's Blaze category series featuring sexier and more explicit love stories. Foster's heroes are sexy but sensitive and always have a very strong honorable streak; in turn her heroines are feisty, sexy, and independent. Foster is also one of the few romance novelists to feature a plus-sized heroine in the novel *Beguiled.*

> *Good looks, great body, intelligence, enthusiasm and money ... Drew Black would be quite the catch if he wasn't such a sexist foul-mouthed jerk with the tact of a mountain goat.*

Lori Foster
Back in Black, 2010

Major Works

Novels in Series by Lori Foster

Winston Brothers and Visitation

Jamie, 2005
Just a Hint—Clint, 2004
When Bruce Met Cyn..., 2004
The Secret Life of Bryan, 2004
Say No to Joe? 2003
Wild, 2001

Brava Brothers

Never Too Much, 2002
Too Much Temptation, 2002

Novels by Lori Foster

The Gift of Love, 2010
Back in Black, 2010
My Man, Michael, 2009
Hard to Handle, 2008
Simon Says, 2007
Causing Havoc, 2007

Murphy's Law, 2006
Jude's Law, 2006
Unexpected, 2003
Casey, 2002
Caught in the Act, 2001
Beguiled, 1999

Category Novels by Lori Foster

Harlequin Temptation

Riley, #930, 2003
Mr. November, #856, 2001
Treat Her Right, #852, 2001
Sex Appeal, #829, 2001
Jordan, #798, 2000

Gabe, #794, 2000
Morgan, #790, 2000
Sawyer, #786, 2000
In Too Deep, #770, 2000
Wanton, #752, 1999

Sizzle: Body Heat, #739,
   1999
Tantalizing, #715, 1999
Taken!, #698, 1998

Fantasy, #675, 1998
Scandalized!, #657, 1997
Outrageous, #629, 1997
Impetuous, #572, 1996

Other Category Novels

Annie, Get Your Guy & Messing Around with Max, Harlequin Duets #47, 2001
Say Yes, Harlequin Duets #23, 2000
Married to the Boss, Maitland Maternity #3, 2000
Little Miss Innocent?, Silhouette Desire #1200, 1999

Novels in Series by L. L. Foster

Servant Series

The Kindred, 2009
The Acceptance, 2008
The Awakening, 2007

Other Works

The Write Ingredients: Recipes from Your Favorite Authors. Samhain Publishing. 2007.
"How to Break the Rules & Get Published." *Writer's Digest,* Volume 80, Issue 12. December 2000. pp. 24–27.
"Quickie with Lori Foster on Criticism." *All About Romance.* May 29, 2000. http://www.likesbooks.com/quick22.html. Last visited December 2009. "Finding Your E-Book Publisher." *Writer's Digest,* Volume 79, Issue 12, December 1999. p. 17.
"Four Facets of a Sparkling Book Proposal." *Writer's Digest,* Volume 79, Issue 10, October 1999. pp. 14–18.

Research Sources

Encyclopedias and Handbooks

"Lori Foster." Literature Resource Center. (subscription database). 2007. http://galenet.galegroup.com/. Last visited December 2009.
Mosley, Shelley and Van Winkle, Sandra. "Lori Foster." In *Romance Today: An A-To-Z Guide to Contemporary American Romance Writers.* Ed. John Charles and Shelley Mosley. Westport, CT: Greenwood, 2007. pp. 114–117.

Biographies and Interviews

"Interview with Lori Foster." *The Impalers—Vampire Band.* February 27, 2008. http://vampireband.blogspot.com/search?q=lori+foster. Last visited December 2009.

"Introducing Lori Foster." *Welcome to Manukau Libraries.* http://www.manukau-libraries.govt.nz/EN/ReadingReviews/Pages/Einterviewwith LoriFoster.aspx. Last visited December 2009.

Osborne, Gwendolyn. "Meet Author Lori Foster." *The Romance Reader.* June 13, 2000. http://www.theromancereader.com/lfoster.html. Last visited December 2009.

Wolfe, Gena. "Lori Foster Interview." *Gena Wolfe.* http://www.genawolfe.com/AuthorPage.html. Last visited December 2009.

Web Site

Lori Foster. http://www.lorifoster.com/. Last visited December 2009. The official Web site for Lori Foster; includes a backlist of titles, an FAQ, biographical information, a newsletter, and a gallery of photographs.

Running with Quills. http://www.runningwithquills.com. Last visited December 2009. Multiauthor newsletter and blog for Foster's fans.

Roberta Gellis (1927–)

Historical / Medieval / Paranormal

Biographical Sketch

Whether they are medieval romances or 19th-century mysteries, Roberta Gellis's novels are noteworthy for their detailed historical research. Even her fantasy novels take place during the past. All of Gellis's stories portray strong characters coping with their time period without the transfer of 21st-century sensibilities. Gellis's books are complex, exquisitely researched, and may cover a character's entire life.

Gellis graduated from Hunter College with a BA, and she furthered her education with an MS in biochemistry from Brooklyn Polytechnic Institute and an MA in medieval literature from New York University. Gellis used her chemistry degree while working as a researcher for Foster D. Snell Inc. and as the science book editor for the McGraw-Hill Book Company. In 1986, Gellis received the Romance Writers of America Lifetime Achievement Award.

> *"Then I must thank your mother," Magdalene said, smiling, "because I am glad you did not drown."*
>
> *"Probably because I was born to be hanged," Bell said lightly...*
>
> Roberta Gellis
Bone of Contention, 2002

Major Works

Novels in Series

Magdalene la Batarde Mysteries

Chains of Folly, 2006
Bone of Contention, 2002
A Personal Devil, 2002
A Mortal Bane, 1999

Roselynde Chronicles

Desiree, 2005
Sybelle, 1983
Rhiannon, 1982
Gulliane, 1980
Joanna, 1979
Alinor, 1978
Roselynde, 1978

The Royal Dynasty or Siren Song

A Silver Mirror, 1989
Fire Song, 1984
Winter Song, 1982
Siren Song, 1981

Tales of Jernaeve

Fires of Winter, 1987
Tapestry of Dreams, 1985

Single Title Novels

Overstars Mail, 2004
Lucrezia Borgia and the Mother of Poisons, 2003
Thrice Bound, 2001
A Delicate Balance, 2000
Bull God, 2000
Enchanted Fire, 1996
Shimmering Splendor, 1995
Dazzling Brightness, 1994
A Delicate Balance, 1993
A Silver Mirror, 1989

Masques of Gold, 1988
The Rope Dancer, 1986
A Woman's Estate, 1984
Fortune's Bride, 1983
The Cornish Heiress, 1981
The English Heiress, 1980
The Sword and the Swan, 1977
The Dragon and the Rose, 1977
Sing Witch, Sing Death, 1975
Bond of Blood, 1965
Knight's Honor, 1964

Novels Written as Priscilla Hamilton

The Love Token, 1979

Novels Written as Max Daniels

Offworld, 1978
The Space Guardian, 1977

Novels Written as Leah Jacobs

The Psychiatrist's Wife, 1966

Collaborations

With Mercedes Lackey

And Less than Kind, 2008
By Slanderous Tongues, 2007
Ill Met by Moonlight, 2005
This Scepter'd Isle, 2004

Other Works

The Dursleys as Social Commentary. In *Mapping the World of Harry Potter: Science Fiction and Fantasy Writers Explore the Bestselling Fantasy Series of All Time.* Ed. Mercedes Lackey and Leah Wilson. Dallas: BenBella Books. 2005.

Research Sources

Encyclopedias and Handbooks

Hamilton-Selway, Joanne. "Roberta Gellis." In *Romance Today: An A-To-Z Guide to Contemporary American Romance Writers.* Ed. John Charles and Shelley Mosley. Westport, CT: Greenwood, 2007. pp. 135–137.

Kemp, Barbara E. "Roberta Gellis." In *Twentieth-Century Romance and Historical Writers.* Ed. Aruna Vasudevan. 3rd ed. London: St. James Press. 1990. pp. 255–257.

"Roberta Gellis." *Literature Resource Center.* (subscription database). 2009. http://galenet.galegroup.com/. Last visited June 2009.

Biographies and Interviews

Falk, Kathryn. "Roberta Gellis." *Love's Leading Ladies.* New York: Pinnacle Books. 1982. pp. 131–135.

"Flycon Interview: Roberta Gellis." *Articulate.* March 15, 2009. http://blogs. abc.net.au/articulate/2009/03/flycon-interv-6.html Last visited August 2009.

Guiley, Rosemary. "Roberta Gellis." *Love Lines: A Romance Reader's Guide to Printed Pleasures.* New York: Facts on File Publications. 1983. pp. 212–214.

Jorgenson, Jane. "Roberta Gellis: A Classic Author Talks About an Expansive Career." All *About Romance.* March 10, 2003. http://www.likesbooks. com/robertagellis.html. Last visited August 2009.

Mason, Jean. "Catching Up with Roberta Gellis." *The Romance Reader.* June 11, 2000. http://www.theromancereader.com/catch-gellis.html. Last visited August 2009.

"Romance ... With a Little Myth-Story!" *PNR: Paraphernalia.* April 2001. http://paranormalromance.org/RobertaGellis.htm. Last visited August 2009.

Weisskopf, Toni. "Interview with Roberta Gellis." *Baen.* January 2005. http://www.baen.com/intgellis.htm. Last visited August 2009.

Web Site

Roberta Gellis. http://www.robertagellis.com/. Last visited December 2009. The official Web site of Roberta Gellis; includes biographical information, a backlist, and links to resources and reference books for historical information.

Rachel Gibson (1962–)

Contemporary

Biographical Sketch

Rachel Gibson was born in Boise, Idaho, is happily married to Mr. G., and has three daughters. A struggling reader all her life, Gibson did not think about becoming a writer until one night she sat down and rewrote the ending to *Gone with the Wind.* She wrote four manuscripts in six years before submitting one to a publisher. That manuscript became the novel *Simply Irresistible.*

Gibson often uses unconventional heroes, such as professional hockey players, that are strong, tough, and rough around the edges, while her heroines are quirky, dynamic, and fun. Her humorous stories often contain connected characters, and minor characters in one book often show up as the hero or heroine in a subsequent story.

> *She was talking about severed heads and stinking carcasses and he was getting turned on. Right there in Handy Man Hardware, like he was six-teen again and couldn't control himself.*
>
> Rachel Gibson
> *Tangled Up in You,* 2007

Major Works

Novels in Series

Writer Series

Another Bad Date, 2008
Tangled Up in You, 2007

I'm in No Mood for Love, 2006
Sex, Lies and Online Dating, 2006

Novels

Nothing But Trouble, 2010
True Love and Other Disasters, 2009
The Trouble with Valentine's Day, 2005
Daisy's Back in Town, 2004
See Jane Score, 2003
Lola Carlyle Reveals All, 2002
True Confessions, 2001
It Must Be Love, 2000
Truly Madly Yours, 1999
Simply Irresistible, 1998

Research Sources

Encyclopedias and Handbooks

"Let's Give a Warm Book Binge Welcome to . . . Rachel Gibson." *Book Binge.* March 19, 2008. http://thebookbinge.com/2008/03/lets-give-warm-book-binge-welcome.html. Last visited August 2009.

Mosley, Shelley and van Winkle, Sandra. "Rachel Gibson." In *Romance Today: An A-To-Z Guide to Contemporary American Romance Writers.* Ed. John Charles and Shelley Mosley. Westport, CT: Greenwood. 2007. pp. 141–144.

"Rachel Gibson." *Literature Resource Center.* (subscription database). 2007. http://galenet.galegroup.com/. Last visited July 2009.

Biographies and Interviews

Coleman, Sandy. "Writer's Corner: Rachel Gibson." *All About Romance* January 20, 2005. http://www.likesbooks.com/gibson.html. Last visited August 2009.

Russell, Jennifer. "August Author of the Month: Rachel Gibson." *The Romance Reader.* http://www.theromancereadersconnection.com/aotm/authorofthe monthgibson.html. Last visited August 2009.

Wolfe, Gena. "Rachel Gibson Interview." *Gena Wolfe.* http://www.genawolfe. com/RachelGibsonInterview.pdf. Last visited August 2009.

Yamashita, Brianna. "A Labor of Love." *Publishers Weekly,* Volume 252, Issue 4, January 26, 2004. p. 237.

Web Sites

Rachel Gibson. http://www.rachelgibson.com/. Last visited December 2009. The official Rachel Gibson Web site includes biographical information, a backlist of her titles, and an FAQ.

The Goddess Blogs

http://thegoddessblogs.com/. Last visited December 2009. A multi-author blog site featuring Rachel Gibson.

Heather Graham / Heather Graham Pozzessere / Shannon Drake (1953–)

Historical / Contemporary / Romantic Suspense / Paranormal

Biographical Sketch

Heather Graham married right after high school and is the mother of five children. After the birth of her third child Graham began her writing career. Graham is a founding member of the Florida chapter of the Romance Writers of America. In 2003 Heather Graham received the Romance Writers of America's Lifetime Achievement Award.

Graham uses the pseudonym of Shannon Drake to differentiate her historic and paranormal novels from her grittier contemporary and romantic suspense novels. With hobbies like boating and scuba diving, Graham brings true realism to her plots.

> *Not that New Orleans was a city where only natives could be found. It was the kind of place people simply fell in love with, as if it had a personality all its own. Of course, some people loathed the city's free and easy spirit and he had to admit, the vomit in the streets after a particularly wild night during Mardi Gras wasn't exactly a selling point.*

Heather Graham
Blood Red, 2007

Major Works

Novels in Series

Bone Island by Heather Graham

Ghost Moon, 2010
Ghost Night, 2010
Ghost Shadow, 2010
Ghost Memories, 2010

Flynn Brother Trilogy by Heather Graham

Deadly Gift, 2008
Deadly Harvest, 2008
Deadly Night, 2008

Suspense Series Written by Heather Graham

The Presence, 2004
Dead on the Dance Floor, 2004
Picture Me Dead, 2003
Hurricane Bay, 2002
Dying to Have Her, 2001
Long, Lean and Lethal, 2000
Tall, Dark and Deadly, 1999
Drop Dead Gorgeous, 1998

Florida Series by Heather Graham

Triumph, 2000
Glory, 1999
Surrender, 1998
Rebel, 1997
Captive, 1996
Runaway, 1994

Civil War Trilogy by Heather Graham

And One Rode West, 1992
And One Wore Gray, 1992
And One Wore Blue, 1991

North American Woman Trilogy by Heather Graham

Love Not a Rebel, 1989
A Pirate's Pleasure, 1989
Sweet Savage Eden, 1989

Viking Trilogy by Heather Graham

Lord of the Wolves, 1993
The Viking's Woman, 1990
Golden Surrender, 1985

The Graham Series Written as Shannon Drake

The Queen's Lady, 2007
When We Touch, 2004
The Lion in Glory, 2003
The Knight Triumphant, 2002
Seize the Dawn, 2001
Conquer the Night, 2000
Come the Morning, 2000

Vampire Series Written by Shannon Drake

Dead by Dusk, 2005
The Awakening, 2003

Realm of the Shadows, 2002
Deep Midnight, 2001
When Darkness Falls, 2000
Beneath a Blood Red Moon, 1999

No Other Series Written by Shannon Drake

No Other Love, 1997
No Other Woman, 1996
No Other Man, 1995

Novels Written as Heather Graham

Night of the Wolves, 2009
Unhallowed Ground, 2009
Dust to Dust, 2009
Nightwalker, 2009
The Death Dealer, 2008
The Last Noel, 2007
The Séance, 2007
Blood Red, 2007
The Dead Room, 2007
Kiss of Darkness, 2006
The Vision, 2006

The Island, 2006
Ghost Walk, 2005
Killing Kelly, 2005
Haunted, 2003
A Season of Miracles, 2002
Night of the Blackbird, 2001
Night Heat, 2001
A Magical Christmas, 1996
Spirit of the Season, 1993
Every Time I Love You, 1988
Devil's Mistress, 1986

Candlelight Ecstasy Romance Novels Written as Heather Graham

Siren From the Sea, #512, 1987
Eden's Spell, #476, 1986
The Maverick and the Lady, #452, 1986
Sensuous Angel, #359, 1985
Hold Close the Memory, #335, 1985

Hours to Cherish, #241, 1984
Tender Deception, #214, 1984
Quiet Walks the Tiger, #177, 1983
A Season for Love, #154, 1983
Tender Taming, #125, 1983
When Next We Love, #117, 1983

Candlelight Ecstasy Supreme Novels Written as Heather Graham

Liar's Moon, #159, 1987
Handful of Dreams, #127, 1986
Dante's Daughter, #108, 1986
An Angel's Share, #94, 1985
Queen of Hearts, #67, 1985
Arabian Nights, #37, 1984
Red Midnight, #17, 1984
Night, Sea, and Stars, #10, 1984
Tempestuous Eden, #1, 1983

Silhouette Intimate Moments Written as Heather Graham

Suspicious, #1379, 2005
In the Dark, #1309, 2004

Novels Written as Heather Graham Pozzessere

Never Sleep with Strangers, 1998
If Looks Could Kill, 1997
Down in New Orleans, 1996
For All of Her Life, 1995
Eyes of Fire, 1995
An Angel's Touch, 1995
Slow Burn, 1994

Silhouette Intimate Moments Written as Heather Graham Pozzesere

The Trouble with Andrew, #525, 1993
Between Roc and a Hard Place, #499, 1993
Mistress of Magic, #450, 1992
Hatfield and McCoy, #416, 1992
Snowfire, #386, 1991
Wedding Bell Blues, #352, 1990
Forever My Love, #340, 1990
A Perilous Eden, #328, 1990
Borrowed Angel, 293, 1989
Lucia in Love, #265, 1988

This Rough Magic, #260, 1988
Angel of Mercy, #248, 1988
Strangers in Paradise, #225, 1988
King of the Castle, #220, 1987
All in the Family, #205, 1987
Bride of the Tiger, #192, 1987
A Matter of Circumstance, #174, 1987
The Game of Love, #165, 1986
Double Entendre, #145, 1986
The di Medici Bride, #132, 1986
Night Moves, #118, 1985

Other Category Titles Written as Heather Graham Pozzessere

The Last Cavalier, Silhouette Shadows #1, 1993

Harlequin Historical Titles Written as Heather Graham Pozzessere

Forbidden Fire, #66, 1991
Apache Summer, #33, 1989
Rides a Hero, #19, 1989
Dark Stranger, #9, 1988

Novels Written as Shannon Drake

The Pirate Bride, 2008
Beguiled, 2006
Reckless, 2006
Wicked, 2005
Kings Pleasure, 1998
Ondine, 1997

Blue Heaven / Black Night, 1995
Branded Hearts, 1995
Tomorrow the Glory, 1994
Lie Down in Roses, 1994
Knight of Fire, 1993

Bride of the Wind, 1992　　　　　　*Emerald Embrace,* 1991
Damsel in Distress, 1992　　　　　*Princess of Fire,* 1989

Research Sources

Encyclopedias and Handbooks

"Heather Graham Pozzessere." *Literature Resource Center.* (subscription database). 2008. http://galenet.galegroup.com/. Last visited June 2009.

Biographies and Interviews

Courtemanche, Dolores. "Romance Writer Heather Graham Creates Romance Novels Amid Hubbub of Family Life." *Worcester Telegram & Gazette.* January 4, 1994.

King-Gamble, Marcia. "Interview with Heather Graham." *Romantically Yours.* February 2005. http://www.theromancewriterslife.com/romantically yours/2005/ry_002.html. Last visited August 2009.

Maughan, Shannon. "Love Is a Many-Splendored Thing." *Publisher's Weekly,* Volume 245, Issue 20, May 19, 1998. p. 45.

Web Site

Heather Graham. http://www.eheathergraham.com/index.htm. Last visited December 2009; a Web site for Heather Graham and Shannon Drake; includes a book list, links to appearances, and a news section.

Original Heather Graham Web site. http://www.theoriginalheathergraham.com/. Last visited December 2009; a Web site devoted to Heather Graham; includes biographical information, a link to appearances, and a list of her books currently in print.

Robin Lee Hatcher / Robin Leigh (1951–)

Inspirational / Historical / Contemporary

Biographical Sketch

Hatcher was born in Idaho and is an accomplished horsewoman. She began her writing career with the story of a sweeping family saga, taking nine months to write the story, and two years later published it as *Stormy Surrender.* Divorced, with two young girls, Hatcher kept her day job for several more years, but finally became a writer full-time.

During the mid-1990s, Hatcher made the switch from historical romance to Christian romance. Several of her older novels have been reworked to reflect Hatcher's Christian values, such as the Coming to America series. Hatcher's heroines are spunky, strong, and intelligent, and her heroes find the love and healing they never knew they needed. A strong relationship with God is a hallmark of any Hatcher character. A past president of the Romance Writers of America, Hatcher received the Lifetime Achievement Award from the Romance Writers of America in 2001.

This bunch of mustangs had been captured off the range in the southwest corner of the state. Wild didn't begin to describe the look in their eyes. They were wary, some scared, a few mean, and none of them wanted to be where they were now, walled in by fences.

Robin Lee Hatcher
Fit to be Tied, 2009

Major Works

Novels in Series by Robin Lee Hatcher

The Sisters of Bethlehem Spring

A Matter of Character, 2010
Fit to be Tied, 2009
A Vote of Confidence, 2009

Burke Family

Return to Me, 2007
A Carol of Christmas, 2006

Hart's Crossing

Home to Hart's Crossing, 2008
Sweet Dreams Drive, 2007
Diamond Place, 2006
Veterans Way, 2005
Legacy Lane, 2004

Coming to America

Promised to Me, 2003
In His Arms, 1998
Patterns of Love, 1998
Dear Lady, 1997

Novels

When Love Blooms, 2009
Bundle of Joy, 2008
Wagered Heart, 2008

Americana Series

Remember When, 1994
Forever, Rose, 1994
Where the Heart Is, 1993

Women West

Devlin's Promise, 1992
Promise Me Spring, 1991
Promised Sunrise, 1990

Spring Haven Saga

Heart Storm, 1986
Heart's Landing, 1984
Stormy Surrender, 1984

The Perfect Life, 2008
Trouble in Paradise, 2007
Another Chance to Love You, 2006

Loving Libby, 2005
The Victory Club, 2005
Beyond the Shadows, 2004
Catching Katie, 2004
Speak to Me of Love, 2003
Firstborn, 2002
Ribbon of Years, 2001
The Shepherd's Voice, 2000
Whispers from Yesterday, 1999
The Forgiving Hour, 1999
Kiss Me, Katie, 1996

Chances Are, 1996
Liberty Blue, 1995
The Magic, 1993
Midnight Rose, 1992
Dream Tide, 1990
The Wager, 1989
Gemfire, 1988
Pirate's Lady, 1987
Passion's Gamble, 1986
Thorn of Love, 1985

Category Novels

Silhouette Special Edition

Daddy Claus, #1288, 1999
Taking Care of the Twins, #1259, 1999
Hometown Girl, #1229, 1999

Novels by Robin Leigh

The Hawk and the Heather, 1992
Rugged Splendor, 1991
Winds of Fire, 1987

Research Sources

Encyclopedias and Handbooks

"Robin Lee Hatcher." *Literature Resource Center.* (subscription database). 2002. http://galenet.galegroup.com/. Last visited June 2009.
van Winkle, Sandra. "Robin Lee Hatcher." In *Romance Today: An A-To-Z Guide to Contemporary American Romance Writers.* Ed. John Charles and Shelley Mosley. Westport, CT: Greenwood. 2007. pp. 162–164.

Biographies and Interviews

Brewer, Rogenna. "An Interview with Author Robin Lee Hatcher." *Heart of Denver Romance Writers.* http://www.hodrw.com/robinleehatcherinterview.htm. Last visited December 2009.
Mills, DiAnn. "Interview: Robin Lee Hatcher." http://www.diannmills.com/int-rlhatcher.html. Last visited December 2009.

"Robin Lee Hatcher." *Christian Book Previews.* http://www.christian book previews.com/christian-book-author-interview.php?isbn=0842355588. Last visited December 2009.

"Robin Lee Hatcher." *Faithful Reader.* February 2004. http://www.faithful reader.com/authors/au-hatcher-robin-lee.asp.Last visited December 2009.

"Robin Lee Hatcher." *Focus on Fiction.* http://www.focusonfiction.net/html/ robinleehatcher.html. Last visited December 2009.

Ward, Jean Marie. "Robin Lee Hatcher: Inspirational Commitment." *Crescent Blues e-Magazine,* Volume 4, Issue 3. http://www.crescentblues. com/4_3issue/int_robin_lee_hatcher.shtml. Last visited December 2009.

"Writer Finds Niche in Christian Genre." *Idaho Statesman.* April 11, 2002.

Criticism and Readers' Guides

"At the Back Fence: Editorial: The Robin Lee Hatcher Fiasco." *All About Romance.* April 21, 2002. http://www.likesbooks.com/editorial.html. Last visited December 2009.

Web Site

Robin Lee Hatcher: Faith. Courage. Love. http://www.robinleehatcher.com/. Last visited December 2009. The official Web site of Robin Lee Hatcher; includes a complete backlist, questions for book clubs, an FAQ, and a media kit.

Candice Hern

Regency / Historical

Biographical Sketch

An early love of Regency fashion, Regency era antiques, and Jane Austen set the stage for Candice Hern's writing career. Hern began writing later in life after discovering Georgette Heyer and Signet Regency novels. After a successful career in marketing, a friend suggested that due to her knowledge of Regency life Hern begin writing Regency romance novels herself. She decided to give it try and in 1995 published her first novel, *A Proper Companion.* Hern graduated from the University of California at Berkley and until recently made her home in the Bay Area. She then moved from Northern California to Minnesota and claims to enjoy the Minnesota winter.

Hern's novels are meticulously researched. On her Web site, she has created an entire "Regency world" with glossaries, fashion plates, collectibles, and a time line. Character development is the most important part of the story for Hern and her heroines, while strong, never forget the era in which they live.

> *"I assure, Aunt Fanny, that though I have reached the ripe old age of six and twenty, I do not feel so very grown up. I haven't done much living, you see, and I have come to London to change that."*
>
> Candice Hern
> *Miss Lacey's Last Fling,* 2001

Major Works

Novels in Series

The Merry Widows Trilogy

Lady Be Bad, 2007
Just One of Those Flings, 2006
In the Thrill of the Night, 2006

The Ladies Fashionable Cabinet Trilogy

Once a Gentleman, 2004
Once a Scoundrel, 2003
Once a Dreamer, 2003

School Companions Trilogy

An Affair of Honor, 1996
A Change of Heart, 1995
A Proper Companion, 1995

Novels

Her Scandalous Affair, 2004
The Bride Sale, 2002
Miss Lacy's Last Fling, 2001
The Best Intentions, 1999
A Garden Folly, 1997

Research Sources

Encyclopedias and Handbooks

"Candice Hern." *Literature Resource Center.* (subscription database). 2007. http://galenet.galegroup.com/. Last visited August 2009.

Charles, John and Hamilton-Selway, Joanne. "Candice Hern." In *Romance Today: An A-To-Z Guide to Contemporary American Romance Writers.* Ed. John Charles and Shelley Mosley. Westport, CT: Greenwood. 2007. pp. 169–172.

Biographies and Interviews

Athitakis, Mark. "That Secret Shame: You Don't Have to be Embarrassed to Read Romance Novels Anymore. *S. F. Weekly,* Volume 20, July 25, 2001.
"Candice Hern, Visiting Vagabond." *Romance Vagabonds.* September 30, 2008. http://www.romancevagabonds.com/?p=1834. Last visited August 2009.
Hughes, Kalen. "Welcome, Candice Hern." *History Hoydens.* August 8, 2007. http://historyhoydens.blogspot.com/2007/08/welcome-candice-hern. html. Last visited August 2009.
Hur, June. "Author Interview: Candice Hern." *Miss Bluestocking.* June 16, 2009. http://missbluestocking.wordpress.com/2009/06/16/author-interview-candice-hern/. Last visited August 2009.
Jefferson, Ambrosia. "Author Interview: Candice Hern." *Fire & Ice.* June 10, 2009. http://www.icewarmth.com/2009/06/author-interview-candice-hern.html. Last visited August 2009.
McCabe, Amanda. "Interview with Candice Hern, Author of *Just One of Those Flings.*" *Risky Regencies.* September 10, 2006. http://riskyregencies. blogspot.com/2006/09/interview-with-candice-hern-author-of.html. Last visited August 2009.

Web Site

Candace Hern Romance Novelist. http://www.candicehern.com/. Last visited December 2009. The official Candace Hern Web site; includes a bookshelf, biographical information, pictures of Hern's regency collection, and a detailed list of links to historical resources.

Georgette Heyer (1902–1974)

Regency / Historical

Biographical Sketch

Georgette Heyer was born in 1902 in the Wimbledon area in London, England. At the age of 17, she wrote her first story as entertainment for her sick brother. In 1925, Heyer married George Ronald Rougier, a mining engineer. His career took the newly married couple to Russia, a few years later to East Africa and then onto Macedonia. Even during her travels, Heyer continued to write, producing a book a year. In 1929, Heyer and family returned to England and Rougier left his job, making Heyer the primary support for the family. Later Rougier studied law and joined the bar in 1939. During World War II and the following years, Heyer continued writing to support her family. Heyer's health began to decline in the 1960s and on July 4, 1974, she passed away.

Besides Regency historical novels, Heyer wrote mystery novels. She alternated her writing during the year, first writing a Regency novel and then switching to a mystery story. Heyer's mystery stories contained the same wit and charm found in her Regency stories.

Heyer's Regency works are the standard for the genre. Her detailed research of the time period was sometimes criticized by critics, but without that research the novels would not be as evocative of the time periods. The way Heyer wove details about the clothing, food, interior design, and her use of Regency slang gave her stories an authentic feel that has not been duplicated. Heyer's study of the Napoleonic Wars, chronicled in *The Infamous Army,* has been used to study military history. In short, Heyer's many Regency stories are considered the classics of the genre by both writers and readers alike.

"Cousin, my uncle Horace informed us that you were a good little thing, who would give us no trouble. You have been with us for rather less than half a day: I shudder to think what havoc you will have wrought by the end of a week."

Georgette Heyer
The Grand Sophy, 1950

Major Works

Novels

My Lord John, 1975	*The Quiet Gentleman,* 1951
Lady of Quality, 1972	*The Grand Sophy,* 1950
Charity Girl, 1970	*Arabella,* 1949
Cousin Kate, 1968	*The Foundling,* 1948
Black Sheep, 1966	*The Reluctant Widow,* 1946
Frederica, 1965	*Friday's Child,* 1944
False Colours, 1963	*Penhallow,* 1942
The Nonesuch, 1962	*Envious Casca,* 1941
A Civil Contract, 1961	*Faro's Daughter,* 1941
The Unknown Ajax, 1959	*The Corinthian,* 1940
Venetia, 1958	*The Spanish Bride,* 1940
Sylvester or the Wicked Uncle, 1957	*No Wind of Blame,* 1939
	A Blunt Instrument, 1938
Sprig Muslin, 1956	*Royal Escape,* 1938
Bath Tangle, 1955	*An Infamous Army,* 1937
The Toll-Gate, 1954	*Behold, Here's Poison,* 1936
Cotillion, 1953	*The Talisman Ring,* 1936
Duplicate Death, 1951	*Death in the Stocks,* 1935

Regency Buck, 1935
The Convenient Marriage, 1934
The Unfinished Clue, 1934
Why Shoot a Butler, 1933
Devil's Cub, 1932
The Conqueror, 1931
Barren Corn, 1930

Beauvallet, 1929
Helen, 1928
The Masqueraders, 1928
These Old Shades, 1926
Simon the Coldheart, 1925
Instead of the Thorn, 1923
The Black Moth, 1921

Research Sources

Encyclopedias and Handbooks

"Georgette Heyer." *Literature Resource Center.* (Subscription database). 2003. http://galenet.galegroup.com/. Last visited June 2009.

Rowland, S. A. "Georgette Heyer." In *Twentieth-Century Romance and Historical Writers.* Ed. Aruna Vasudevan. 3rd ed. London: St. James Press. 1990. pp. 309–311.

Womack, Kenneth. "Georgette Heyer." In *Dictionary of Literary Biography: British Novelists Between the Wars.* Detroit, MI: Gale Research. 1998. pp. 183–189.

Biographies and Interviews

"Georgette Heyer Is Dead at 71: Wrote Regency England Novels." *New York Times.* July 6, 1974. p. 20.

Hodge, Jane Aiken. *The Private World of Georgette Heyer.* London: Bodley Head. 1984.

"Obituaries: Miss Georgette Heyer." *Times.* July 6, 1974. p. 14.

Criticism and Readers' Guides

Andrews, Beth. "So Violent a Fancy: Georgette Heyer Mysteries." *Mystery Scene,* Volume 97, 2006. pp. 18–20.

Bargainier, Earl F. "The Dozen Mysteries of Georgette Heyer." *Clues: A Journal of Detection,* Volume 3, Issue 2, Fall–Winter 1982. pp. 30–39.

Chris, Teresa. *Georgette Heyer's Regency England.* London: Sidgwick & Jackson. 1989.

Devlin, James P. "A Janeite's Life of Crime: The Mysteries of Georgette Heyer." *Arm Chair Dective: A Quarterly Journal Devoted to the Appreciation of Mystery, Detective, and Suspense Fiction,* Volume 17, Issue 3, Summer 1984. pp. 300–315.

Fahnestock-Thomas, Mary. *Georgette Heyer: A Critical Retrospective.* Saraland, AL: PrinnyWorld Press. 2001.

Fletcher, Lisa. *Historical Romance Fiction: Heterosexuality and Performativity.* Alde, England: Ashgate. 2008.

Kloester, Jennifer. *Georgette Heyer's Regency World.* London: William Heinemann. 2005.

Townsend, Juliet. "The High-Kick of Regency Fashion." *Spectator,* Volume 295, Issue 9178, July 3, 2004. pp. 41.

Wallace, Diana. "History to the Defeated: Women Writers and the Historical Novel in the Thirties." *Critical Survey,* Volume 15, Issue 2, May 2003. pp. 76–92.

Westman, Karin E. "A Story of Her Weaving: The Self-Authoring Heroines of Georgette Heyer's Regency Romance." In *Doubled Plots: Romance and History.* Ed. Susan Strehle and Mary Paniccia Carden. Jackson: University Press of Mississippi. 2003. pp. 165–184.

Web Sites

The Definitive Fan Web Site for Georgette Heyer. http://www.georgette-heyer.com/index.html. Last visited December 2009. A fan Web site providing a biography, a list of works, information about the Regency world, and a reading list.

Georgette Heyer. http://www.colby.edu/personal/l/leosborn/heyer/. Last visited December 2009. Web site devoted to the published works of Heyer. Provides links to publishing dates for British and U.S. editions, and a gallery of original cover art.

Linda Howard (1950–)

Contemporary | Romantic Suspense | Historical | Paranormal | Category

Biographical Sketch

Linda Howington uses the pseudonym Linda Howard for her many novels. From the age of nine, Howard knew she wanted be a writer. She attended community college to become a journalist but quickly decided she would like to write her own stories. After 20 years of practice she submitted her first novel to Silhouette and was published. Married to professional Bass master fisherman Gary Howington, Howard travels with her husband and maintains her writing schedule on the road. All of her life, she has lived in the same county in Alabama with her large extended family.

Howard's stories are fast-paced with independent females and strong, dominant male heroes who are everyday people living extraordinary lives. Humor also plays a large role in her novels.

He'd never thought he would love any woman, least of all an Anglo, but that was before this slight, delicate creature had bulldozed her way into his life and completely changed it. He could no more live without her now than he could live without air.

Linda Howard
Mackenzie's Mountain, 1989

Major Works

Novels

Veil of Night, 2010
Ice, 2010
Burn, 2009
Death Angel, 2008
Up Close and Dangerous,
    2007
Drop Dead Gorgeous, 2006
Killing Time, 2005
To Die For, 2005
Kiss Me While I Sleep, 2004
Cry No More, 2003
Dying to Please, 2002

Open Season, 2001
Mr. Perfect, 2000
All the Queen's Men, 1999
Now You See Her, 1998
Son of the Morning, 1997
Shades of Twilight, 1996
After the Night, 1995
Dream Man, 1995
Heart of Fire, 1993
The Touch of Fire, 1992
Angel Creek, 1991
A Lady of the West, 1990

Category Novels

Silhouette Intimate Moments

A Game of Chance, #1021, 2000
Mackenzie's Pleasure, #691, 1996
Loving Evangeline, #607, 1994
Against the Rules, #22, 1983
Mackenzie's Mission, #445, 1992
Duncan's Bride, #349, 1990

Mackenzie's Mountain, #281,
    1989
Heartbreaker, #201, 1987
Diamond Bay, #177, 1987
Midnight Rainbow, #129, 1986
Tears of the Renegade, #92, 1985

Silhouette Special Edition

White Lies, #452, 1988
Almost Forever, #327, 1986
The Cutting Edge, #260, 1985
Sarah's Child, #230, 1985
Come Lie with Me, #177, 1984
An Independent Wife, #46, 1982
All That Glitters, #22, 1982

Nocturne Series

Raintree: Inferno, #15, 2007

Research Sources

Encyclopedias and Handbooks

Kemp, Barbara. "Linda Howard." In *Twentieth-Century Romance and Histori-cal Writers.* Ed. Aruna Vasudevan. 3rd ed. London: St. James Press. 1990. pp. 327–328.

"Linda Howard." *Literature Resource Center.* (subscription database). 2008. http://galenet.galegroup.com/. Last visited August 2009.

Biographies and Interviews

Coleman, Sandy. "Writer's Corner: Linda Howard." *All About Romance.* December 2004. http://www.likesbooks.com/howard2004.html. Last visited August 2009.

"Linda Howard—Who Knew." *All About Romance.* August 11, 2000. http://www.likesbooks.com/lindahoward.html. Last visited August 2009.

Lodge, Sally. "Linda Howard: Preferred Fiction to Journalism." *Publisher's Weekly,* Volume 245, Issue 20, May 18, 1998. p. 46.

Vido, Jennifer. "Interview with Linda Howard." *Jen's Jewels.* July 15, 2008. http://freshfiction.com/page.php?id=1140. Last visited August 2009.

Ward, Jean Marie. "Linda Howard: Men in Uniform and Magic Dust." *Crescent Blues e-Magazine*, Volume 4, Issue 3. http://www.crescentblues.com/4_3issue/int_Linda_howard.shtml. Last visited August 2009.

Web Site

Author Spotlight: Linda Howard. http://www.randomhouse.com/author/results.pperl?authorid=35941. Last visited December 2009. The Random House publishers webpage contains brief biographical information and a list of her more recent titles.

If You Like Linda Howard

Linda Howard's novels feature male heroes who are emotionally scared and have to learn to trust in love. Due to the hero's fear of love, he often treats the heroine cruelly and the heroines in a Howard novel generally prove to be stronger than the heroes. Howard's stories are tight, emotional, and some of the best romantic suspense stories published.

You May Like

Suzanne Brockmann

Suzanne Brockmann writes action, adventure, and romantic suspense romance novels. Her stories feature military men of action who find love in unexpected places. In turn, her heroines are as tough as the heroes, with emotional scars much like those possessed by heroes in other romance novels. Fast-paced action and smart dialogue make a Brockman novel a fun read.

Nora Roberts Writing as J. D. Robb

J. D. Robb writes futuristic, romantic suspense novels. Her stories feature Eve Dallas as a homicide detective who along with her husband Roarke solve the mystery every time. Witty dialogue and fast-paced action make any Robb (or Roberts book for that matter) an enjoyable read.

Sharon Sala

Sharon Sala writes gritty, realistic, romantic suspense stories that demonstrate that love can exist in a dangerous world. Her characters, all of whom have a core belief in God, give the stories depth and strong appeal and her heroines are flawed but strong.

Judith Ivory / Judy Cuevas

Historical Novels

Biographical Sketch

Judith Ivory is the pseudonym used by Judy Cuevas, who has written historical romances under both names. The switch from Cuevas to Ivory was made at the request of the publisher when she switched publishing houses. Ivory, who has multiple degrees in applied and theoretical mathematics, was a math teacher at the high school level and then a professor at the University of Miami before she began writing full-time.

Ivory's historical novels mostly take place during the Victorian era, a time frame not often used in Romance. The heroines in her works are often uncommon women, either courtesans or working women, while the heroes may be younger than the heroines or from a different social level.

> *The huge house was like a picture that had been hanging a few degrees off center. It came into proper focus—unique and rich, made up of myriad idiosyncratic details—only after it had been touched by the right hand.*
>
> Judith Ivory
> *Angel in a Red Dress,* 2006

Major Works

Novels Written as Judith Ivory

Angel in a Red Dress, 2006 (reprint of *Starlit Surrender*)
Untie My Heart, 2002
The Indiscretion, 2001
The Proposition, 1999
Sleeping Beauty, 1998
Beast, 1997

Novels Written as Judy Cuevas

Dance, 1996
Bliss, 1995

Black Silk, 1991
Starlit Surrender, 1988

Other Works

Ivory, Judith. "Judith Ivory Answers Your Questions." *All About Romance.* May 10, 2000. http://www.likesbooks.com/ivory2.html. Last visited August 2009.
Cuevas, Judy. "On Writing, Art, Issues, and Publishing in Spite of it All." In *North American Romance Writers.* Ed. Kay Mussell and Johanna Tunon. London: Scarecrow Press. 1999. pp. 53–58.

Research Sources

Biographies and Interviews

Coleman, Sandy. Writer's Corner: Historical Romance Roundtable. *All About Romance.* September 2004. http://www.likesbooks.com/histroundtable. html. Last visited August 2009.
Irvin, Carol. "Covers Covered by Carol: The Long, Long Cover Journal from Judy Cuevas to Judith Ivory." *All About Romance.* February 8, 2000. http://www.likesbooks.com/covrcol13.html. Last visited August 2009.
"Judith Ivory: Intelligence That Shines Through." *All About Romance.* March 22, 1999. http://www.likesbooks.com/ivory.html. Last visited August 2009.
Ward, Jean Marie. "Judith Ivory: Passionate Victorian." *Crescent Blues e-Magazine.* Volume 2, Issue 6. http://www.crescentblues.com/2_6issue/ivory. shtml. Last visited August 2009.

Web Site

Judith Ivory. http://www.booktalk.com/jivory/index.htm. Last visited December 2009. Judith Ivory's Web site provides biographical information and a list of her titles.

Karin Kallmaker / Laura Adams (1960–)

Contemporary / Historical / Lesbian / Paranormal

Biographical Sketch

Karin Kallmaker used the pseudonym Laura Adams for her science fiction and fantasy titles, and Karin Kallmaker for her Romance titles. Kallmaker was born in Sacramento, California, and received a bachelor's degree in business from California State University Sacramento. Kallmaker is currently the editorial director for Bella Books, a well-known publisher of lesbian fiction.

Kallmaker's stories are rich with character development, with real-life women working to overcome a tragedy, who find love when they least expect it. Works that Kallmaker categorizes as erotica have realistic characters and engaging plots, which is different from many erotic stories.

> Some time later, Lisa grunted and said, "Not a bad story. And I got stood up."
> "Whoever she is, she's a fool."
> Lisa looked up from the magazine. "That's the nicest thing you've ever said to me."
> Ani continued giving most of her attention to an article on fly fishing near Bristol Bay. "Don't get used to it."

Karin Kallmaker
Warming Trend, 2009

Major Works

Novels in Series

Rayann Series

Watermark, 1999
Touchwood, 1991

Novels by Karin Kallmaker

Above Temptation, 2010
Stepping Stone, 2009
Warming Trend, 2009
The Kiss That Counted, 2008
18th & Castro, 2006
Finders Keepers, 2006
Just Like That, 2005
Sugar, 2004
One Degree of Separation, 2004
Frosting on the Cake, 2003

Maybe Next Time, 2003
Substitute for Love, 2001
Unforgettable, 2000
Making Up for Lost Time, 1998
Embrace in Motion, 1997
Wild Things, 1996
Painted Moon, 1994
Car Pool, 1993
Paperback Romance, 1992
In Every Port, 1990

Novels in Series by Laura Adams

Tunnel of Light

Seeds of Fire, 2002
Sleight of Hand, 2001

Novels by Laura Adams

The Dawning, 1999
Christabel: A Novel, 1998
Night Vision, 1997

Research Sources

Biographies and Interviews

Kriegh, LeeAnn. "In Their Own Words: Part 1: Karin Kallmaker." *After Ellen.com.* May 26, 2008. http://www.afterellen.com/books/2008/5/their own words_part1?page=0%2C5. Last visited December 2009.

Parks, Joy. "Q Syndicate—Interview by Joy Parks. *Romance & Chocolates.* May 4, 2006. http://kallmaker.blogspot.com/2006/05/q-syndicate-inter view-by-joy-parks.html. Last visited December 2009.

Web Sites

Karin Kallmaker. http://www.kallmaker.com/. Last visited December 2009. The official Web site of Karin Kallmaker; includes a list of current books, contact information, a calendar of appearances, and a link to her publisher's discussion board.

Romance & Chocolate: Writing, Reading, and Lesbians. http://kallmaker.blog spot.com/search/label/Stepping%20Stone. Last visited December 2009. The official blog of Karin Kallmaker.

Lisa Kleypas (1964–)

Historical / Contemporary

Biographical Sketch

Lisa Kleypas is a graduate of Wellesley College in Wellesley, Massachusetts with a degree in political science. In 1985, she was crowned Miss Massachusetts and competed in the Miss America pageant in Atlantic City. A longtime reader of romance novels, Kleypas sold her first novel at the age of 21. The rest, as they say, is history. She has penned 25 novels, primarily historicals. In 2007 Kleypas made the switch from historical to contemporary, with the publication of *Sugar Daddy.*

Kleypas's novels are filled with smart, nontraditional characters and although many of her historical novels take place during the Regency era, they are not the "novel of manners" books that dominate the genre. The Wallflower series shifts the historical period from the Regency to the Victorian time frame. Her titles are about overcoming fear through the power of love.

This was too much. Daisy Bowman was furious because he hadn't done the thing he had craved and dreamed of for years of his life. He had behaved honorably, damn it all, and instead of being appreciative she was angry.

Lisa Kleypas
Scandal in Spring, 2006

Major Works

Novels in Series

Hathaway Family

Love in the Afternoon, 2010
Married by Morning, 2010
Tempt Me at Twilight, 2009
Seduce Me at Sunrise, 2008
Mine Till Midnight, 2007

Wallflowers Series

Scandal in Spring, 2006
Devil in Winter, 2006
It Happened One Autumn, 2005
Secrets of a Summer Night, 2004

Bow Street Runner Series

Worth Any Price, 2003
Lady Sophia's Lover, 2002
Someone to Watch Over Me, 1999

Single Title Novels

Blue-Eyed Devil, 2008
Sugar Daddy, 2007
Again the Magic, 2004
Where's My Hero, 2003
When Strangers Marry, 2002
Suddenly You, 2001
Where Dreams Begin, 2000
Stranger in My Arms, 1998
Because You're Mine, 1997
Somewhere I'll Find You, 1996

Prince of Dreams, 1995
Midnight Angel, 1995
Dreaming of You, 1994
Then Came You, 1993
Only with Your Love, 1992
Only in Your Arms, 1992
Give Me Tonight, 1989
Forever My Love, 1988
Love, Come to Me, 1988
Where Passion Leads, 1987

Research Sources

Encyclopedias and Handbooks

"Lisa Kleypas." *Literature Resource Center.* (subscription database). 2008. http://galenet.galegroup.com./ Last visited December 2009.

Biographies and Interviews

Coleman, Sandy. "Lisa Kleypas." *All About Romance.* May 2006. http://www. likesbooks.com/kleypasint.html. Last visited March, 2008.

Coleman, Sandy. "Lisa Kleypas: This Author has Legs." *All About Romance.* March 15, 2004. http://www.likesbooks.com/kleypas.html. Last visited March, 2008.

Klose, Stephanie. "Lisa Kleypas' Modern Love: Historical Author Publishes Her First Contemporary Romance." *Romantic Times,* #277. May 25, 2006.

Reed, S. "Lisa Kleypas, New Wellesley Grad, Beauty Queen (gasp!) and Successful Romance Novelist." *People Weekly,* Volume 28, Issue 20, November 16, 1987. pp. 139–140.

White, C. E. "A Conversation with Lisa Kleypas." *Writers Write: The Internet Writing Journal.* December 1998. http://www.writerswrite.com/journal/dec98/kleypas.htm .Last visited March 2008.

Web Site

Lisa Kleypas. http://www.lisakleypas.com/index.asp. Last visited December 2009. Kleypas's official Web site. Provides excerpts from her most recent titles, biographical information, a list of characters who appear in multiple books, and a gallery of photos.

Jayne Ann Krentz / Amanda Quick / Jayne Castle / Stephanie James / Jayne Bentley / Jayne Taylor / Amanda Glass (1948–)

Contemporary / Historical / Paranormal / Futuristic

Biographical Sketch

Jayne Ann Krentz writes contemporary novels and romantic suspense novels under her own name and uses pseudonyms to write in other subgenres of romance. She uses "Amanda Quick" for historical novels and "Jayne Castle," Krentz's maiden name, for futuristic, science fiction romances. In turn, she published short, contemporary novels under "Stephanie James" and has also used "Jayne Bentley," "Jayne Taylor," and "Amanda Glass" for a few category titles.

Krentz has a bachelor's degree in history from the University of California, Santa Cruz, and a master's in library science from San Jose State University. The day she graduated from library school, Krentz married Frank Krentz and they have spent over 30 years together. In 2007 Krentz established the Castle Humanities Fund at the University of California, Santa Cruz, to support the library. Krentz and her husband have lived in the Seattle area since the 1970s.

No matter what name Krentz uses, her later stories usually include paranormal elements. Krentz is an unabashed proponent of the alpha hero, and her heroines are equally strong-willed. Most of her stories have a strong family element in the form of a biological family or of close friends. In 1995 Krentz was received the Lifetime Achievement Award from the Romance Writers of America.

> *"I thought you were going to offer something else."*
> *"My lush, lovely, nubile body?"*
> *Stark cleared his throat. "That thought did cross my mind."*
> *"Tacky, Stark, very, very tacky."*

Jayne Ann Krentz
Trust Me, 1995

Major Works

Novels in Series

Arcane Society

Midnight Crystal, 2010 (by Jayne Castle)
Burning Lamp, 2010 (by Amanda Quick)
Fired Up, 2009 (by Jayne Ann Krentz)
The Perfect Poison, 2009 (by Amanda Quick)
Running Hot, 2009 (by Jayne Ann Krentz)
The Third Circle, 2008 (by Amanda Quick)
Sizzle and Burn, 2008 (by Jayne Ann Krentz)
White Lies, 2007(by Jayne Ann Krentz)
Second Sight, 2006 (by Amanda Quick)

Whispering Springs by Jayne Ann Krentz

Truth or Dare, 2004
Light in Shadow, 2003

Eclipse Bay by Jayne Krentz

Summer in Eclipse Bay, 2002
Dawn in Eclipse Bay, 2001
Eclipse Bay, 2000

Vanza Series by Amanda Quick

Lie by Moonlight, 2005
Wicked Widow, 2000
I Thee Wed, 1999

Lavinia Lake and Tobias March Books by Amanda Quick

Late for the Wedding, 2003
Don't Look Back, 2002
Slightly Shady, 2001

Harmony Series by Jayne Castle

Obsidian Prey, 2009
Dark Light, 2008
Silver Master, 2007
Ghost Hunter, 2006
After Glow, 2004
After Dark, 2000

Curtain—Futuristic World of St. Helen's by Jayne Castle

Orchid, 1998
Zinnia, 1997
Amaryllis, 1996

Guinevere Jones by Jayne Castle

The Fatal Fortune, 1986
The Sinister Touch, 1986
The Chilling Deception, 1986
The Desperate Game, 1986

Novels Written as Jayne Ann Krentz

All Night Long, 2006
Falling Awake, 2004
Smoke in Mirrors, 2002
Lost & Found, 2001
Soft Focus, 1999
Eye of the Beholder, 1999
Flash, 1998
Sharp Edges, 1998
Deep Waters, 1997
Absolutely, Positively, 1996
Trust Me, 1995
Grand Passion, 1994
Hidden Talents, 1993

Wildest Hearts, 1993
Family Man, 1992
Perfect Partners, 1992
Sweet Fortune, 1991
Silver Linings, 1991
Golden Chance, 1990
Gift of Fire, 1989
Gift of Gold, 1988
Midnight Jewels, 1987
A Coral Kiss, 1987
Crystal Flame, 1986
Sweet Starfire, 1986
Twist of Fate, 1986

Category Novels Written as Jayne Ann Krentz

Harlequin Temptation Written as Jayne Ann Krentz

The Private Eye, #377, 1992
The Wedding Night, #365, 1991
Too Wild to Wed?, #341, 1991
The Cowboy, #302, 1990
The Adventurer, #293, 1990
The Pirate, #287, 1990

Lady's Choice, #270, 1989
A Woman's Touch, #241, 1989
Dreams, Part Two, #230, 1988
Dreams, Part One, #229, 1988
Joy, #219, 1988
Full Bloom, #191, 1988

The Chance of a Lifetime, #168, 1987
The Main Attraction, #157, 1987
The Family Way, #146, 1987
Between the Lines, #125, 1986
The Ties That Bind, #109, 1986
True Colors, #91, 1986

Witchcraft, #74, 1985
Man with a Past, #45, 1985
Ghost of a Chance, #34, 1985
Call it Destiny, #21, 1984
Uneasy Alliance, #11, 1984

Harlequin Intrigue Written as Jayne Ann Krentz

Legacy, #10, 1985
The Waiting Game, #17, 1985

Novels Written as Amanda Quick

The River Knows, 2007
Wait Until Midnight, 2005
The Paid Companion, 2004
With This Ring, 1998
Affair, 1997
Mischief, 1996
Mystique, 1995
Mistress, 1994
Desire, 1994

Deception, 1993
Dangerous, 1993
Reckless, 1992
Ravished, 1992
Rendezvous, 1991
Scandal, 1991
Surrender, 1990
Seduction, 1990

Novels Written as Jayne Castle

Trading Secrets, 1985
Double Dealing, 1984

Candle Light Ecstasy Romance Written as Jayne Castle

Conflict of Interest, #130, 1983
Spellbound, #91, 1982
Power Play, #79, 1982
A Negotiated Surrender, #68, 1982
Affair of Risk, #55, 1982
Relentless Adversary, #45, 1982

A Man's Protection, #36, 1982
Bargain with the Devil, #26, 1981
Right of Possession, #23, 1981
Wagered Weekend, #17, 1981
Gentle Pirate, #2, 1980

McFadden Series Written as Jayne Castle

Vintage of Surrender, #132, 1979
Queen of Hearts, #157, 1979

Silhouette Desire Written as Stephanie James

Saxon's Lady, unnumbered, 1987
The Challoner Bride, #342, 1987
Second Wife, #307, 1986
Green Fire, #277, 1986

Cautious Lover, #253, 1986
Golden Goddess, #235, 1985
Wizard, #211, 1985
The Devil to Pay, #187, 1985

Night of the Magician, #145, 1984
Fabulous Beast, #127, 1984
Gambler's Woman, #115, 1984
Body Guard, #103, 1983
Battle Prize, #97, 1983
The Silver Snare, #85, 1983
Gamemaster, #67, 1983
To Tame the Hunter, #55, 1983

Affair of Honor, #49, 1983
Price of Surrender, #37, 1983
Reckless Passion, #31, 1982
Renaissance Man, #25, 1982
Lover in Pursuit, #19, 1982
Velvet Touch, #11, 1982
Corporate Affair, #1, 1982

Other Category Titles Written as Stephanie James

Raven's Prey, Silhouette Intimate Moments #21, 1984
Serpent in Paradise, Silhouette Intimate Moments, #9, 1983
Stormy Challenge, Silhouette Special Edition #35, 1982
Dangerous Magic, Silhouette Special Edition #15, 1982
A Passionate Business, Silhouette Romance #89, 1981

Category Novels Written as Jayne Bentley

McFadden Series

Sabrina's Scheme, #283, 1979
Hired Husband, #274, 1979
Maiden of the Morning, #249, 1979
Turning Towards Home, #224, 1979
A Moment Past Midnight, #192, 1979

Novels Written as Amanda Glass

Shield's Lady, 1989

Novels Written as Jayne Taylor

Whirlwind Courtship, 1979

Other Works

Krentz, Jayne Ann. *Are We There Yet? Mainstreaming the Romance.* Keynote
   Speech, Bowling Green State University Conference on Romance. August
   2000. http://www.krentz-quick.com/bgspeech.html. Last visited August
   2009.
Editor, *Dangerous Men and Adventurous Women: Romance Writers on the
   Appeal of the Romance,* 1992.

Research Sources

Encyclopedias and Handbooks

Charles, John, Mosley, Shelley, Hamilton-Selway, Joanne, and van Winkle,
   Sandra. "Jayne Ann Krentz." In *Romance Today: An A-To-Z Guide to*

Contemporary American Romance Writers. Ed. John Charles and Shelley Mosley. Westport, CT: Greenwood. 2007. pp. 217–224.

"Jayne Ann Krentz." *Literature Resource Center.* (subscription database). 2008. http://galenet.galegroup.com/. Last visited June 2009.

Kemp, Barbara. "Jayne Ann Krentz." In *Twentieth-Century Romance and Historical Writers.* Ed. Aruna Vasudevan. 3rd ed. London: St. James Press. 1990. pp. 374–375.

Biographies and Interviews

Albers, Lisa. "Romancing the Tome." *Seattle Woman Magazine.* February 2008. http://www.seattlewomanmagazine.com/articles/feb08–2.htm. Last visited September 2009.

"ARR Interview with Jayne Ann Krentz." *A Romance Review.* January 2006. http://www.aromancereview.com/interviews/jayneannkrentz.phtml. Last visited August 2009.

Brighton, Lori. "Interview with Jayne Ann Krentz." *Lori Brighton Online Journal.* April 25, 2009. http://loribrighton.blogspot.com/2009/04/interview-with-jayne-ann-krentz.html. Last visited August 2009.

Falk, Kathryn. "Jayne Castle." *Love's Leading Ladies.* New York: Pinnacle Books. 1982. pp. 53–56.

Guiley, Rosemary. "Jayne Castle." *Love Lines: A Romance Reader's Guide to Printed Pleasures.* New York: Facts on File Publications. 1983. pp. 201–203.

Mussell, Kay. "Paradoxa Interview with Jayne Ann Krentz." *Paradoxa,* Volume 3, Issue 1–2, 1997. pp. 46–57.

Paget, Ruth Pennington. "Interview with Jayne Ann Krentz." *San Jose State University SLIS Alumni News,* Volume 7, Issue 1, Spring 2005. https://slisgroups.sjsu.edu/alumni/joomla/index.php?option=com_content&task=view&id=27&Itemid=305#ijk. Last visited August 2009.

Patterson, Lezlie. "Love Really Does Conquer All." *McClatchy—Tribune Business News.* February 13, 2007. Last visited August 2009.

Samuel, Barbara. "Q&A." *BookPage.* http://www.bookpage.com/books-14096-White+Lies?PHPSESSID=f3b2aa17f83ed6c9c8b4fc7c99b7dc6f. Last visited August 2009.

Scharf, Michael. "Conflict Management: How It's Done (Darkly, This Time), Romantic Suspense-Style: PW Talks to Jayne Ann Krentz." *Publishers Weekly,* Volume 252, Issue 48, December 5, 2005. p. 28.

Webster, Dan. "Jayne Ann Krentz." *SpokesmanReview.* September 6, 2009. http://www.spokesmanreview.com/interactive/bookclub/interviews/interview.asp?IntID=17. Last visited August 2009.

White, Claire E. "A Conversation with Jayne Ann Krentz." *Writers Write: The Internet Writing Journal.* http://www.writerswrite.com/journal/dec02/krentz.htm. Last visited August 2009.

Wilson, Angela. "Virtual Sitdown with Jayne Ann Krentz." *Pop Syndicate.* January 5, 2009. http://www.popsyndicate.com/books/story/virtual_sitdown_with_jayne_ann_krentz. Last visited August 2009.

"The Writing Raw.com 7 Question Interview." *Writing Raw.* http://writingraw. com/files/7%20Question%20Interview%20with%20Jayne%20Ann%20 Krentz.pdf. Last visited August 2009.

Criticism and Readers' Guides

Fera-VanGent, Tania. *Popular Romance Novels: Seeking Out the 'Sisterhood.'* Master's Thesis, Brock University. 2007.
Therrien, Kathleen Mary. *Trembling at Her Own Response: Resistance and Reconciliation in Mass-Market Romance Novels.* PhD Dissertation. University of Delaware. 1997.

Web Sites

Jayne Ann Krentz. http://www.krentz-quick.com/. Last visited December 2009. The official webpage for Krentz; includes a complete book list, information about the Arcane Society, contests, biographical information, and links to romance-friendly bookstores.
Running with Quills. http://www.runningwithquills.com./ Last visited December 2009. Multiauthor newsletter and blog for fans of Krentz.

If You Like Jayne Ann Krentz

Krentz (under her own name and her pseudonyms) writes in many genres, featuring a variety of time periods and characters. More recent Krentz novels include both mystery and paranormal elements. Krentz's novels feature strong male heroes, and heroines who are strong and smart enough to keep up with the hero, as well as, a strong connection to family or a family of friends.

You May Like

Johanna Lindsey

Johanna Lindsey's historical novels, especially the Malory Family series center on strong characters who will risk almost anything for love. Lindsey's novels cover the medieval period, Regency period, the Old West and futuristic time periods. Lindsey is one of the most successful romance writers from the late 20th century.

Susan Elizabeth Phillips

Susan Elizabeth Phillips writes stories that feature heroines who are less than perfect heroines and strong males who work hard to get what they want. Humor is always a key element in any Philips novel; moreover, Philips is one of the few romance authors to use professional athletes as heroes.

Nora Roberts

Nora Robert's more recent novels feature fast-paced action and romantic suspense as well as her trademark witty dialogue. Although, the heroes may be more sensitive than the dominant heroes of the past, their sensitivity adds to, rather than detracts from, their strength of character. In turn, her heroines are smart, determined, and looking for happiness.

Christina Skye

Christina Sky writes connected stories in her Draycott Abbey and Code Name series. While the characters are strong, honorable, and smart, the heroines are usually professionals with real careers in unlikely fields whom the heroes find themselves very protective of.

Stephanie Laurens
Historical / Regency
Biographical Sketch

Stephanie Laurens was born in Ceylon, now known as Sri Lanka, and moved with her family to Australia at the age of five. She attended the University of Melbourne and graduated with a PhD in biochemistry. After graduation, Laurens and her husband moved to England, where she was a cancer research scientist. Four years later, Laurens and her husband returned to Australia. After running out of romance novels to read, she decided to try her hand at writing one. Her first novel sold, and Laurens decided to make the switch from scientific research to romance. Laurens and her husband continue to live in Melbourne, Australia.

Her stories all take place during the time frame of the Regency period, but while they take place in the *ton* they never have the stuffy feeling of some Regency stories. Laurens's heroes are all strong, men who like control—the masters of their households. The heroines are strong and confident enough to never allow the heroes to dominate them. While the stories may take place during the Regency time frame, Laurens's novels are very sensual and occasionally humorous.

> *She was stranded in a cottage with a dying man and man known as Devil.*
>
> Stephanie Laurens
> *Devil's Bride,* 1998

Major Works
Novels in Series

Black Cobra Quartet
Black Cobra Quartet #3: The Brazen Bride, 2010

Black Cobra Quartet #2: The Elusive Bride, 2010
Black Cobra Quartet #1: The Untamed Bride, 2009

Bar Cynster

Temptation and Surrender, 2009
The Taste of Innocence, 2007
What Price Love, 2006
The Truth About Love, 2005
The Ideal Bride, 2004
The Perfect Lover, 2003
On a Wicked Dawn, 2002
On a Wild Night, 2002

The Promise in a Kiss, 2001
All About Passion, 2001
All About Love, 2001
A Secret Love, 2000
A Rogue's Proposal, 1999
Scandal's Bride, 1999
A Rake's Vow, 1998
Devil's Bride, 1998

Bastion Club

Mastered by Love, 2009
The Edge of Desire, 2008
Beyond Seduction, 2007
To Distraction, 2006
A Fine Passion, 2005
A Lady of His Own, 2004
A Gentleman's Honor, 2003
The Lady Chosen, 2003
Captain Jack's Woman, 1997

Novels

Where the Heart Leads: The Casebook of Barnaby Adair, 2008

Category Novels

Harlequin Historical

A Comfortable Wife, #45, 1997
An Unwilling Conquest, #41, 1996
A Lady of Expectations, #37, 1995
The Reasons for Marriage, #33, 1994
Four in Hand, #25, 1994
Impetuous Innocent, #19, 1994
Fair Juno, #13, 1994
Tangled Reins, #3, 1992

Other Works

Essays

"The Hero as Pursuer." *Stephanie Laurens.com.* http://www.stephanielaurens.com/Library_Article2.htm. Last visited August 2009.

Keynote Address: Librarians' Day, Romance Writers of America. July 29, 2008. *Stephanie Laurens.*com. http://www.stephanielaurens.com/Library_RWA_Librarians_keynote.htm. Last visited August 2009.

"Why Set Romances in the Regency?" Stephanie Laurens.com. http://www.stephanielaurens.com/Press_Article1.html. Last visited August 2009.

Research Sources

Encyclopedias and Handbooks

"Stephanie Laurens." *Literature Resource Center.* (subscription database). 2008. http://galenet.galegroup.com/. Last visited August 2009.

Biographies and Interviews

"Author Interview: Stephanie Laurens." *HarperCollins.* http://www.harpercollins.com/author/authorExtra.aspx?authorID=17367&displayType=interview. Last visited August 2009.

Smith, Kathryn. "5 Questions With . . . Stephanie Laurens." *Avon Authors.* January 24, 2009. http://www.avonauthors.com/5-questions-withstephanie-laurens/. Last visited August 2009.

White, Claire E. "Interview with Stephanie Laurens." *Writers Write: The Internet Writing Journal.* http://www.writerswrite.com/journal/feb98/laurens.htm. Last visited August 2009.

White Claire E. "A Conversation with Stephanie Laurens." *Writers Write: The Internet Writing Journal.* April 2004. http://www.writerswrite.com/journal/apr04/laurens2.htm. Last visited August 2009.

Wolfe, Gena. "Stephanie Laurens Interview." *Gena Wolfe.* http://www.genawolfe.com/StephanieLaurensInterview.pdf. Last visited August 2009.

Web Site

Stephanie Laurens http://www.stephanielaurens.com/index.htm. Last visited December 2001; Lauren's official Web site; includes biographical information, complete back list of titles, information about the Cynster family and the Bastion Club, and a newsletter.

Johanna Lindsey (1952–)

Historical / Western / Medieval / Futuristic

Biographical Sketch

Johanna Lindsey has written some of the best-loved novels of the romance genre, and for many years, was one of the few romance authors to be published in mainstream fiction. Born in Germany to a military father and homemaker mother, Lindsey and her mother settled in Hawaii after her father's death, where she married young and had three children. On a whim, she began writing romance novels like those she enjoyed reading. Currently, Lindsey lives in New England.

Lindsey's stories feature strong males and females. As her catalogue of works has grown, her heroines have become a bit younger and spunkier. Lindsey's stories also cover a lot different eras in time, several of which are set in exotic locales, including Russia, the American West, Regency England, and medieval England.

"Now you have to deal with me. Get your goddamn hands off my woman."

Johanna Lindsey
A Heart So Wild, 1986

Major Works

Novels in Series

Reid Family

A Rogue of My Own, 2009
The Devil Who Tamed Her, 2007
The Heir, 2000

Malory-Anderson Families

That Perfect Someone, 2010
No Choice But Seduction, 2008
Captive of My Desires, 2006
A Loving Scoundrel, 2004
The Present, 1998
Say You Love Me, 1996
The Magic of You, 1993
Gentle Rogue, 1990
Tender Rebel, 1988
Love Only Once, 1985

Straton Family

All I Need is You, 1997
A Heart So Wild, 1986

Sherring Cross

The Pursuit, 2002
Love Me Forever, 1995
Man of My Dreams, 1992

Shefford's Knights

Joining, 1999
Defy Not the Heart, 1989

Ly-San-Ter

Heart of a Warrior, 2001
Keeper of the Heart, 1993
Warrior's Woman, 1990

Cadinia's Royal Family

You Belong to Me, 1994
Once a Princess, 1991

Southern Series

Heart of Thunder, 1983
Glorious Angel, 1982

Wyoming Series

Angel, 1992
Savage Thunder, 1989
Brave the Wild Wind, 1984

Haardrad Family

Surrender My Love, 1994
Hearts Aflame, 1987
Fires of Winter, 1980

Novels

Marriage Most Scandalous, 2005
A Man to Call My Own, 2003
Home for the Holidays, 2000
The Heir, 2000
Until Forever, 1995
Man of My Dreams, 1992
Prisoner of My Desire, 1991
Silver Angel, 1988
Secret Fire, 1987

When Love Awaits, 1986
Love Only Once, 1985
Tender is the Storm, 1985
A Gentle Feuding, 1984
So Speaks the Heart, 1983
Paradise Wild, 1981
A Pirate's Love, 1978
Captive Bride, 1977

Research Sources

Encyclopedias and Handbooks

"Johanna Lindsey." *Literature Resource Center.* (subscription database). 2008. http://galenet.galegroup.com./ Last visited August 2009.

Biographies and Interviews

Falk, Kathryn. "Johanna Lindsey." *Love's Leading Ladies.* New York: Pinnacle Books. 1982. pp. 173–176.

"History in the Making: Johanna Lindsey Speaks." *Amazon.com.* http://www. amazon.com/exec/obidos/tg/feature/-/11495/104–0653242–1578367.Last visited September 2009.

Rozen, Leah. "Isn't It Romantic." *Women's Day,* Volume 56, Issue 1, November 24, 1992.

Criticism and Literary Guides

Boyd, Maggie. "At the Back Yard Fence: Authors at Their Best: Everybody Loves a Lindsey." *All About Romance.* November 1, 2004. http://www. likesbooks.com/190.html. Last visited September 2009.

Colemnero, Laura Elizabeth. *The Social Construction of Gender as Represented in Popular Fiction,* 1990–1997. PhD Dissertation. South Dakota State University. 1999.

Web Site

Johanna Lindsey at Harper Collins. http://www.harpercollins.com/author/micro site/?authorid=15195. Last visited December 2009. The publisher's Web site for Lindsey; includes a brief biography and a list of books currently in print.

If You Like Johanna Lindsey

Johanna Lindsey's historical novels, especially the Malory Family series, center on strong characters who will risk almost anything for love. Lindsey's novels cover the medieval period, Regency period, the Old West, and futuristic time periods. Lindsey is one of the most successful romance writers from the late 20th century.

You May Like

Loretta Chase

Loretta Chase writes Regency- and Victorian-era stories that are rigorously researched. Her heroes are damaged emotionally and feel they cannot love. Her heroines are strong women who find love is worth the risk. Chase's stories are always entertaining.

Jayne Anne Krentz

Krentz publishes novels in a number of genres under both her own name and her various pseudonyms. Regardless of genre, many of these novels contain both mystery and paranormal elements, along with strong heroes and smart heroines.

Stephanie Laurens

Laurens's stories are character-driven and feature dominant male heroes, and heroines who are confident enough to stand up to them. While the stories take place during the Regency time period and can be emotional, they are not stuffy. Laurens's stories are all very sensual and can be humorous.

Elizabeth Lowell

Lowell writes the dominant male hero as rough and tough as the readers will allow. Her medieval and contemporary stories feature heroes who never thought of love and heroines who can convince the hero that love can exist.

Nora Roberts

Roberts writes fast-paced, character-driven stories. Her heroines are competent women willing to take risks for love, and her heroes are strong males who want to protect the women they love. Family is a strong feature in almost all of Roberts's works. While her earlier works are lighter, her more recent stories usually have a romantic suspense element.

Bertrice Small

Bertrice Small's historical romances feature strong heroines who take on the historical male roles of running estates or businesses. The plots of her novels accommodate the actual historical facts of the time periods they are set in rather than the reverse and her characters' stories often extend between more than one novel. Small's *Skye O'Malley* novels are considered classics in historical romance.

Cathie Linz

Contemporary / Category

Biographical Sketch

Realizing that what she really wanted to do was write, Cathie Linz, a former acquisitions librarian at a Chicago-area law school, left the academic world to write romance novels. Her first book took six months to write and was published within a year. In 2006, Linz moved from writing shorter, category novels to longer single title stories.

Linz's novels are humorous, fun, and charming. No big angst or serial killers are to be found in these stories. The heroines are smart and unconventional and Linz is one of the few authors to feature a plus-sized heroine (Leena in *Big Girls Don't Cry*). In turn, her heroes can appreciate those unconventional heroines. Linz was awarded an honorary lifetime membership in the Romance Writers of America. She continues to live in Chicago.

> Emma wanted to rebel. She also wanted peace and an end to global warming, but it didn't appear that any of those things were about to happen anytime soon.

Cathie Linz
Smart Girls Think Twice, 2009

Major Works

Novels in Series

Girls Series

Smart Girls Think Twice, 2009
Big Girls Don't Cry, 2007
Bad Girls Don't, 2006
Good Girls Do, 2006

Novels

Mad, Bad and Blonde, 2010

Category Novels

Silhouette Romance

Lone Star Marine, #1805, 2006
The Marine and Me, #1793, 2005
The Marine Meets His Match, #1736,
    2004
Cinderella's Sweet-Talking Marine,
    #1727, 2004
Her Millionaire Marine, #1720, 2004
Sleeping Beauty & the Marine, #1637,
    2003

Married to a Marine, #1616, 2002
A Prince at Last, #1584, 2002
The Marine & the Princess, #1561,
    2001
Stranded with the Sergeant, #1534,
    2001
Daddy in Dress Blues, #1470, 2000
One of a Kind Marriage, #1032, 1994

Harlequin Duets

Between the Covers, #48, 2001
The Lawman Gets Lucky, #26, 2000
The Cowboy Finds a Bride, #17, 1999
The Rancher Gets Hitched, #9, 1999

Silhouette Desire

Husband Needed, #1098, 1997
Abbie and the Cowboy, #1036, 1996
Seducing Hunter, #1029, 1996
Michael's Baby, #1023, 1996
A Wife in Time, #958, 1995
Bridal Blues, #894, 1994
Midnight Ice, #846, 1994
Escapades, #804, 1993
Male Ordered Bride, #761, 1993

Flirting with Trouble, #722, 1992
Smooth Sailing, #665, 1991
Handyman, #616, 1991
Smiles, #575, 1990
Adam's Way, #519, 1989
As Good as Gold, #484, 1989
A Friend in Need, #443, 1988
Change of Heart, #408, 1988

Candelight Ecstasy

A Handful of Trouble, #482, 1987
Lover and Deceiver, #394, 1986
Tender Guardian, #364, 1985
A Glimpse of Paradise, #330, 1985
Pride and Joy, #313, 1985
Winner Takes All, #266, 1984

A Private Account, #242, 1984
A Charming Strategy, #203, 1984
A Summer Embrace, #178, 1983
Wildfire, #157, 1983
Remembrance of Love, #52, 1982

Other Category Titles

Too Smart for Marriage, Harlequin Love & Laughter #51, 1998
Too Sexy for Marriage, Harlequin Love & Laughter #39, 1998
Baby Wanted, Montana Mavericks Series #10, 1995
Continental Lover, Candlelight Ecstasy Supreme #130, 1986

Other Works

Romantic Hearts: A Personal Reference for Romance Readers. Ed. Peggy Jae-
gly. 3rd Edition. Lanham, MD: Scarecrow Press. 1997. pp. 74–75.
"Setting the Stage: Facts and Figures." *Dangerous Men and Adventurous
Women: Romance Writers on the Appeal of the Romance.* Ed. Jayne
Ann Krentz. Philadelphia: University of Pennsylvania Press. 1992.
pp. 13–16.

Research Sources

Encyclopedias and Handbooks

"Cathie Linz." *Literature Resource Center.* (subscription database). 2005.
http://galenet.galegroup.com/. Last visited June 2009.
Charles, John, "Cathie Linz." In *Romance Today: An A-To-Z Guide to Contemporary American Romance Writers.* Ed. John Charles and Shelley
Mosley. Westport, CT: Greenwood. 2007. pp. 237–239.

Biographies and Interviews

Housley, Suzie. "A Writer with Many Hidden Talents: An Interview with
Cathie Linz." *Beneath the Covers Past.* November 2002. http://www.
my shelf.com/beneaththecovers/02/linz.htm. Last visited September
2009.
"Interview with Cathie Linz." *Die Romantische Bueherecke.* http://www.
die-buecherecke.de/linz.htm. Last visited September 2009.

Web Site

Cathie Linz. http://cathielinz.com/. Last visited December 2009. Cathie Linz's official Web site; includes biographical information, a backlist of her novels, and information for her fans.

Elizabeth Lowell / Ann Maxwell / A. E. Maxwell (1944–)

Romantic Suspense / Historical / Medieval / Contemporary / Category

Biographical Sketch

Elizabeth Lowell and A. E. Maxwell are pseudonyms for Ann Maxwell, who was born in Wisconsin and graduated from the University of California with a bachelor's degree. She married Evan Maxwell and now lives in the Pacific Northwest.

Maxwell credits Jayne Ann Krentz for her move from science fiction and mystery to romance. Maxwell's heroes are the definitive, dominant male, many of which have had previously bad experiences with women, while the heroines are strong, young women who help the heroes learn to trust in love. Her stories are emotional and occasionally violent.

> *Spring heals winter's wounds, but spring is rarely a gentle time. The wounds of winter are starkly revealed before they are healed by spring, and only the most hardy of living things survive renewal. Healing is not for the faint of heart.*

> Elizabeth Lowell
> *Untamed,* 1993

Major Works

Novels in Series

St. Kilda Consulting

Death Echo, 2010
Blue Smoke and Murder, 2008
Innocent as Sin, 2007
The Wrong Hostage, 2006

The Donovans

Midnight in Ruby Bayou, 2000
Pearl Cove, 1999
Jade Island, 1998
Amber Beach, 1997

Only Series

Winter Fire, 1996
Autumn Lover, 1996
Only Love, 1995
Only You, 1992
Only Mine, 1992
Only His, 1991

Rarities Unlimited

Die in Plain Sight, 2003
Running Scared, 2002
Moving Target, 2001

Medieval Series

Enchanted, 1994
Forbidden, 1993
Untamed, 1993

Risk Ltd. Written as Ann Maxwell

Shadow and Silk, 1997
The Ruby, 1995

Fiddler and Fiora Mystery Written as Ann Maxwell

Murder Hurts: A Fiddler and Fiora Mystery, 1993
The King of Nothing: A Fiddler and Fiora Mystery, 1992
Money Burns: A Fiddler and Fiora Mystery, 1991
The Art of Survival: A Fiddler and Fiora Mystery, 1989
Just Enough Light to Kill: A Fiddler and Fiora Mystery, 1988
Gatsy's Vineyard: A Fiddler and Fiora Mystery, 1987
The Frog and the Scorpion: A Fiddler and Fiora Mystery, 1986
Just Another Day in Paradise: A Fiddler and Fiora Mystery, 1985

Novels Written as Elizabeth Lowell

Whirlpool (rewrite of *The Ruby*), 2006
Always Time to Die, 2005

Death is Forever (rewrite of *The Diamond Tiger*), 2004
The Color of Death, 2004
Tell Me No Lies, 1986

Category Novels Written as Elizabeth Lowell

Silhouette Desire

Warrior, #631, 1991
Granite Man, #625, 1991
Outlaw, #624, 1991
Fire and Rain, #546, 1990
Dark Fire, #462, 1988

Fever, #415, 1988
Love Song for a Raven, #355, 1987
Too Hot to Handle, #319, 1986
The Fire of Spring, #265, 1986
Summer Thunder, #77, 1983

Silhouette Intimate Moments

Chain Lightning, #256, 1988
Sweet Wind, Wild Wind, #178,
    1987
Fires of Eden, #141, 1986
Sequel, #128, 1986
Valley of the Sun, #109, 1985

Travelling Man, #97, 1985
A Woman Without Lies, #81, 1985
Forget Me Not, #72, 1984
Summer Games, #57, 1984
Lover in the Rough, #34, 1983
The Danvers Touch, #18, 1983

Harlequin Historicals

Reckless Love, #38, 1990

Novels Written as Ann Maxwell

The Secret Sister, 1993
The Diamond Tiger, 1992
Timeshadow Rider, 1986
Name of the Shadow, 1984
Dancer's Illusion, 1983
Dancer's Luck, 1983

Fire Dancer, 1982
The Jaws of Menx, 1981
A Dead God Dancing, 1979
The Singer Enigma, 1976
Change, 1975

Novels Written as A. E. Maxwell

Steal the Sun, 1983
The Golden Mountain, 1990
Golden Empire, 1979

Other Works

"Love Conquers All: The Warrior Hero and the Affirmation of Love." *Dangerous Men and Adventurous Women: Romance Writers on the Appeal of the Romance.* Ed. Jayne Ann Krentz. Philadelphia: University of Pennsylvania Press. 1992. pp. 109–120.

Research Sources

Encyclopedias and Handbooks

"Ann Elizabeth Maxwell." *Literature Resource Center.* (subscription database). 2008. http://galenet.galegroup.com/. Last visited June 2009.

Biographies and Interviews

Dyer, Lucinda. "Elizabeth Lowell: Winning the Trench Warfare." *Publisher's Weekly,* Volume 245, Issue 20, May 18, 1998. p. 49.
"Harper Collins Bestseller Elizabeth Lowell Illuminates the Shadowy World of Art Fraud." *Science Letter.* May 20, 2009. p. 215.
Wehr, Isolde. " Interview with Elizabeth Lowell." *Die Romantische Bucherecke.* April 2001. http://www.die-buecherecke.de/lowell2.htm. Last visited September 2009.
White, Claire E. "A Conversation with Elizabeth Lowell." *Writers Write.* September 2000. http://www.writerswrite.com/journal/sep00/lowell.htm. Last visited September 2009.

Criticism and Readers' Guides

"At the Back Fence #173." *All About Romance.* January 1, 2004. http://www.likesbooks.com/173.html. Last visited September 2009.
"Laurie's News & Views, Issue #73." *Laurie Likes Books.* May 15, 1999. http://www.likesbooks.com/73.html. Last visited September 2009.

Web Sites

Elizabeth Lowell. http://www.elizabethlowell.com. Last visited December 2009. Official Web site of Lowell, includes biographical information, a complete backlist of titles, an FAQ, and notable quotes from her novels.
Running with Quills. http://www.runningwithquills.com. Last visited December 2009. Multiauthor newsletter and blog for fans of Lowell.

Debbie Macomber (1948–)

Contemporary / Category

Biographical Sketch

Debbie Macomber began writing on a rented typewriter in her kitchen when her four children were still young. Although writing was complicated for Macomber by her dyslexia, she persevered and sold her first book, *Heartsong,* after five years of working on it, in 1982. Macomber has been married to her husband Wayne for over 40 years and lives in Port Orchard, Washington.

Macomber's books focus on family, especially on women and how they cope in difficult situations. The relationship Macomber has with her readers is very important to her and she was one of the first authors to include her mailing address in all her books. The importance of Macomber's readers is demonstrated in the role that their feedback has played in creating the Cedar Grove series and Blossom Street series. Her more recent works are moving away from the traditional romance genre and focus more on the friendships of women and less on romance.

> *"I'm not sure. It sounds right." Anne Marie shrugged lightly. The number had leaped into her head, and didn't know quite why. Twenty. Twenty wishes that would help her recapture her excitement about life. Twenty dreams written down. Twenty possibilities that would give her a reason to look forward to the future instead of staying mired in her grief.*

Debbie Macomber
Twenty Wishes, 2009

Major Works

Novels in Series

Cedar Cove

92 Pacific Boulevard, 2009
A Cedar Cove Christmas, 2008
8 Sandpiper Way, 2008
74 Seaside Avenue, 2007
6 Rainier Drive, 2006

50 Harbor Street, 2005
44 Cranberry Point, 2004
311 Pelican Court, 2003
204 Rosewood Lane, 2002
16 Lighthouse Road, 2001

Blossom Street

Summer on Blossom Street, 2009
Twenty Wishes, 2008
Back on Blossom Street, 2007

A Good Yarn, 2005
The Shop on Blossom Street, 2004

Angelic Intervention

Where Angels Go, 2007
Those Christmas Angels, Harlequin Super Romance #1164, 2003
Shirley, Goodness & Mercy, 1999
Can This Be Christmas, 1998
Mrs. Miracle, 1996
Touched by Angels, 1995
The Trouble with Angels, 1994
A Season of Angels, 1993

Heart of Texas

Return to Promise, 2000
Promise, Texas, 1999
Lone Star Baby, 1998
Nells' Cowboy, 1998
Dr. Texas, 1998
Texas Two Step, 1998
Lonesome Cowboy, 1998

Dakota Series

Buffalo Valley, 2001
Always Dakota, 2001
Dakota Home, 2000

Novels

Hannah's List, 2010
The Perfect Christmas, 2009
Christmas Letters, 2006
Susannah's Garden, 2006
There's Something About Christmas, 2005
When Christmas Comes, 2004
The Snow Bride, 2003
Changing Habits, 2002
The Christmas Basket, 2002

Between Friends, 2002
Thursdays at Eight, 2001
Moon Over Water, 1999
Montana, 1998
This Matter of Marriage, 1997
Sooner or Later, 1996
Someday Soon, 1995
One Night, 1994
Morning Comes Softly, 1993

Category Novels

Silhouette Special Edition

Navy Husband #1693, 2005
Just Married #1003, 1996

Same Time, Next Year #937, 1995
Baby Blessed #895, 1994

Marriage Wanted! #842, 1993
Bride Wanted! #836, 1993
Groom Wanted! #831, 1993
Hasty Wedding #798, 1993
Bride on the Loose #756, 1992
Stand-In Wife #744, 1992
Marriage of Inconvenience #732, 1992
Navy Baby #697, 1991
Navy Woman #683, 1991
Navy Brat #662, 1991
The Sheriff Takes a Wife #637, 1990
The Cowboy's Lady #626, 1990

The Courtship of Carol Sommars #606, 1990
Fallen Angel #577, 1989
Denim & Diamonds #570, 1989
For All My Tomorrows #530, 1989
Navy Blues #518, 1989
Navy Wife #494, 1988
The Playboy and the Widow #482, 1988
All Things Considered #392, 1987
White Lace and Promises #322, 1986
Reflections of Yesterday #284, 1986
Borrowed Dreams #241, 1985
Starlight #128, 1983

Silhouette Romance

The Bachelor Prince #1012, 1994
The Way to a Man's Heart #671, 1989
Almost an Angel #629, 1989
Any Sunday #603, 1988
Almost Paradise #579, 1988
Some Kind of Wonderful #567, 1988
Cindy and the Prince #555, 1988
Mail Order Bride #539, 1987
Love 'n Marriage #522, 1987
No Competition #512, 1987
Sugar & Spice #494, 1987
Friends and Then Some #474, 1986

Yesterday Once More #461, 1986
Jury of His Peers #449, 1986
Laughter in the Rain #437, 1986
Yesterday's Hero #426, 1986
Shadow Chasing #415, 1986
Christmas Masquerade #405, 1985
A Friend or Two #392, 1985
The Trouble with Cassi #379, 1985
Adam's Image #349, 1985
Promise Me Forever #341, 1985
That Wintry Feeling #316, 1984

Silhouette Inspirations

Love Thy Neighbor #29, 1985
The Gift of Christmas #23, 1984
Thanksgiving Prayer #21, 1984
A Girl Like Janet #15, 1984
Undercover Dreamer #9, 1984
Heartsong #1, 1984

Harlequin Romance

Ending in Marriage #3403, 1996
Falling for Him #3399, 1996
Because of the Baby #3395, 1996
Daddy's Little Helper #3387, 1995
Marriage Risk #3383, 1995

Brides for Brothers #3379, 1995
Ready for Marriage #3307, 1994
Ready for Romance #3288, 1993
Lone Star Lovin' #3271, 1993
Norah #3244, 1993

Stephanie #3239, 1992
Valerie #3232, 1992
The Man You'll Marry #3196, 1992
My Hero #3180, 1992
The Forgetful Bride #3166, 1991
Here Comes Trouble #3148, 1991
Father's Day #3130, 1991

First Comes Marriage #3113, 1991
Rainy Day Kisses #3076, 1990
Country Bride #3059, 1990
A Little Bit Country #3038, 1990
Yours and Mine #2993, 1989
Love by Degree #2835, 1987
The Matchmakers #2768, 1986

Other Category Novels

The Wyoming Kid, Harlequin American Romance #1121, 2006
Wanted: Perfect Partner, Silhouette Yours Truly #1, 1995

Other Works

Books

One Simple Act: Discovering the Power of Generosity, 2009
Debbie Macomber's Cedar Cove Cookbook, 2009
Knit Together: Discover God's Pattern for Your Life, 2007

Essays

"Why I Write…" *Publisher's Weekly*, Volume 256, Issue 21, May 15, 2009. p. 31.
"7 Trend Tips." *Writer's Digest*, Volume 88, Issue 5, October 2008. p. 46.
With Eykelhot, Paula. "Romancing the Store." *Publisher's Weekly*, Volume 253, Issue 30, July 31, 2006. p. 82.

Movie Based on the Novel of Debbie Macomber

Turner, Brad, director. *This Matter of Marriage*, made for TV movie. February 14, 1998. Internet Movie Database, http://www.imdb.com/title/tt0140615/. Last visited July 2009.

Research Sources

Encyclopedias and Handbooks

"Debbie Macomber." *Literature Resource Center.* (subscription database). 2009. http://galenet.galegroup.com/. Last visited July 2009.
Mosley, Shelly and Van Winkle, Sandra. "Debbie Macomber." In *Romance Today: An A-To-Z Guide to Contemporary American Romance Writers.* Ed. John Charles and Shelley Mosley. Westport, CT: Greenwood. 2007. pp. 248–253.

Biographies and Interviews

Baker, Janda. "Debbie Macomber." *The Writer,* Volume 119, Issue 8, August 2006. p. 66.

Dyer, Lucinda. "Debbie Macomber: Her Dance Card is Filling Up." *Publisher's Weekly,* Volume 245, Issue 20, May 18, 1998. pp. 49–50.

Frank, Dorothea Benton. "Lists, Wishes, and a Little Help from a Reader." *Publisher's Weekly,* Volume 255, Issue 13, March 31, 2008. p. 36.

Huseby, Sandy. "Q&A: Macomber's High-Flying Romance." *Book Page: America's Book Review.* December 2005. http://www.bookpage.com/0512bp/debbie_macomber.html. Last visited July 2009.

Jaegly, Peggy. "Debbie Macomber." *Romantic Hearts: A Personal Reference for Romance Readers.* 3rd ed. Lanham, MD: Scarecrow Press. 1997. pp. 76–77.

Teicher, Craig Morgan. "Debbie Macomber." *Publisher's Weekly.* Volume 253, Issue 30, July 30, 2007. pp. 28.

Criticism and Readers' Guides

Donahue, Dick and Coffey, Michael. "How They Do Debbie." *Publisher's Weekly,* Volume 253, Issue 25, June 19, 2006. pp. 31–34.

Web Site

Debbie Macomber. http://www.debbiemacomber.com/. Last visited December 2009. Debbie Macomber's official Web site; includes a complete backlist with publication dates, biographical information, information for knitters, recipes from her books, and readers' guides for book clubs.

Judith McNaught (1944–)

Historical / Contemporary / Romantic Suspense / Medieval

Biographical Sketch

Judith McNaught, one of the first well-known authors of historical novels, is also one of the first romance authors to make the move from paperbacks to hardcover. Her popularity is largely due to her characters who react to situations much more naturally than most romance characters. Moreover, her heroes, with their exterior hardness, but underlying sensitivity, were the precursors to the modern sensitive romance heroes.

McNaught was born in California and received a bachelor's degree from Northwestern University in business administration. After her first marriage ended, she held a series of jobs in radio and film. It was while working for a film company that she met and married her second husband, Michael Mc-Naught, and subsequently, found her passion for writing romance novels.

> *"It must have been terribly lonely for you growing up," he said sympatheti-cally.*
>
> *"Not at all. Two of my father's wives were nearly as young as I was. I played with them."*

Judith McNaught
Someone to Watch Over Me, 2003

Major Works

Novels in Series

Westmoreland Dynasty

Can't Take My Eyes Off of You, 2010
Until You, 1994
A Kingdom of Dreams, 1989
Whitney, My Love, 1985

Paradise Series

Every Breath You Take, 2005
Night Whispers, 1998
Perfect, 1993
Paradise, 1991

Sequels Series

Almost Heaven, 1990
Something Wonderful, 1988
Once and Always, 1987

Novels

Someone to Watch Over Me, 2003
Remember When, 1996

Category Novels

Double Standards, Harlequin Temptation, #16, 1984
Tender Triumph, Harlequin Super Romance #86, 1983

Research Sources

Encyclopedias and Handbooks

"Judith McNaught." *Literature Resource Center.* (subscription database). 2008. http://galenet.galegroup.com/. Last visited July 2009.

Kemp, Barbara. "Judith McNaught." In *Twentieth-Century Romance and Historical Writers*. Ed. Aruna Vasudevan. 3rd ed. London: St. James Press. 1990. pp. 447–448.

Biographies and Interviews

"A Q & A with Judith McNaught." *All About Romance.* September 7, 1999. http://www.likesbooks.com/mcnaught.html. Last visited September 2009.

Coleman, Sandy. "Writer's Corner: Judith McNaught." *All About Romance.* January 2006. http://www.likesbooks.com/mcnaught2006.html. Last visited September 2009.

Hubbard, Kim and Markley, Debbie. "Queen of Hearts." *People,* Volume 46, Issue 24, December 9, 1996. pp. 83–84.

Sowers, Leslie. "The 'Perfect' Romantic: Judith McNaught Lives Up to Image Put Forth in Her Books." *Houston Chronicle.* July 11, 1993.

Web Site

Judith McNaught. http://www.judithmcnaught.com/. Last visited December 2009. Judith McNaught's official webpage; includes a backlist of novels, a discussion board, and information about her latest release.

Teresa Medeiros (1962–)

Historical / Medieval / Paranormal

Biographical Sketch

Like many Army brats, Teresa Medeiros was born abroad, while her father, a member of the army and her mother, a stay-at-home mom, were stationed in Germany. An only child, Medeiros was a voracious reader. Medeiros graduated from Madisonville Community College with a degree in nursing, and while working as a nurse, Medeiros began writing the kind of books she wanted to read.

Medeiros's stories make you laugh and cry. Rather than restricting herself to one time period, she sets her novels in a variety of time periods, including 123 A.D., 1200s, Regency England, and the current day. Her heroines are spunky and fun while her heroes are strong but sensitive.

Pamela brought her hands together in a round of dry applause. "Bravo, sir! I was wrong about you. Your passion adds a stirring note of conviction to your dialogue. If your weapon didn't happen to be pointed at my heart, I might even be tempted to cheer on your noble effort to relieve me of my purse."

Teresa Medeiros
Some Like it Wild, 2009

Major Works

Novels in Series

Kincaid Highland

Some Like it Wild, 2009
Some Like it Wicked, 2008

Kane/Cabot Vampire

The Vampire Who Loved Me, 2006
After Midnight, 2005

The Fairleigh Sisters

One Night of Scandal, 2003
A Kiss to Remember, 2002

Lenox Family Magic

Touch of Enchantment, 1997
Breath of Magic, 1996

Novels

The Devil Wears Plaid, 2010
Yours Until Dawn, 2004
The Bride and the Beast, 2001
Charming the Prince, 1999
Nobody's Darling, 1998
Fairest of Them All, 1995

Thief of Hearts, 1994
A Whisper of Roses, 1993
Once an Angel, 1993
Heather and Velvet, 1992
Shadows and Lace, 1990
Lady of Conquest, 1989

Research Sources

Encyclopedias and Handbooks

Charles, John. "Teresa Medeiros." In *Romance Today: An A-To-Z Guide to Contemporary American Romance Writers.* Ed. John Charles and Shelley Mosley. Westport, CT: Greenwood. 2007. pp. 270–273.

"Teresa Medeiros." *Literature Resource Center.* (subscription database). 2007. http://galenet.galegroup.com/. Last visited June 2009.

Biographies and Interviews

"Debbie's Den: Sharing Some Time in the Den This Month is Teresa Medeiros." *A Romance Review.* August 2003. http://www.aromancereview.com/debden/den0803.phtml. Last visited September 2009.

Micheletti, Ellen. "Teresa Medeiros: Romance and the Unknown." *All About Romance.* February 22, 1999. http://www.likesbooks.com/medeirosint.html. Last visited September 2009.

Weiss, Angela. "Interview with Teresa Medeiros." *Die Romantische Bucherecke.* April 2000. http://www.die-buecherecke.de/medeirs2.htm. Last visited September 2009.

Web Site

Teresa Medeiros. http://www.teresamedeiros.com/. Last visited December 2009. Teresa Medieros's official Web site, includes biographical information, a backlist of titles, photos of Medeiros, and information for the media.

Kasey Michaels / Michelle Kasey (1943–)

Regency / Historical / Contemporary

Biographical Sketch

Kasey Michaels and Michelle Kasey are the pseudonyms of Kathryn Seidick, who began her writing career just after her oldest son was diagnosed with kidney failure. While caring for him in the hospital, she noticed that the nurses and other mothers of sick children were reading romance novels. She wrote her second book, *The Tenacious Miss Tamerlane,* for those mothers and nurses. Fortunately, the kidney transplant was a success, and Michaels now lives outside Philadelphia with her husband. Her four grown children live nearby.

Michaels writes laugh-out-loud funny novels. Her heroes seldom take themselves too seriously, and when they do, the heroines are there to bring them back to earth. Michaels's humor largely comes through in the dialogue between the characters. While Michaels's contemporary stories may take on a more serious note than her Regencies, she still leaves you with a story that can make you feel good, no matter what kind of day you've had.

> *"You may not be fat or bald, your lordship . . . but you neglected to mention that you possess all the charm and personality of a turnip."*
>
> Michelle Kasey
> *The Beleaguered Lord Bourne,* 1985

Major Works

Series Novels Written as Kasey Michaels

Daughtry Family

How to Beguile a Beauty, 2010
How to Tame a Lady, 2009
How to Tempt a Duke, 2009

Sunshine Girls Romantic Caper

Mischief 24/7, 2009
Dial M for Mischief, 2008
Mischief Becomes Her, 2008

Romney Marsh

Becket's Last Stand, 2007
Return of the Prodigal, 2007
A Reckless Beauty, 2007
A Most Unsuitable Groom, 2007
Beware of Virtuous Women, 2006
The Dangerous Debutante, 2006
A Gentleman By Any Other Name, 2006

Maggie Kelly Books

Bowled Over, 2007
High Heels and Holidays, 2006
High Heels and Homicide, 2005
Maggie Without a Clue, 2004
Maggie by the Book, 2003
Maggie Needs an Alibi, 2002

Trehan Brothers

Be My Baby Tonight, 2002
Love to Love You Baby, 2001

London Friends

Then Comes Marriage, 2002
Someone to Love, 2001
Indiscreet, 1998

Crown Family

The Promise, 1997
The Untamed, 1996
The Homecoming, 1996

Novels

Lords of Scandal, 2009
Lords of Notoriety, 2009
Everything's Coming Up Rosie, 2006
Stuck in Shangri-La, 2005
Shall We Dance, 2005
The Butler Did It, 2004
This Can't Be Love, 2004
The Kissing Game, 2003

This Must be Love, 2003
Can't Take My Eyes Off of You, 2000
Waiting for You, 2000
Come Near Me, 2000
Escapade, 1999
The Secrets of the Heart, 1995
The Passion of an Angel, 1995
The Illusions of Love, 1994
A Masquerade in the Moonlight, 1994
Bride of the Unicorn, 1993
The Legacy of the Rose, 1992
Out of the Blue, 1992
The Wagered Miss Winslow, 1992

The Haunted Miss Hampshire, 1992
The Chaotic Miss Crispino, 1991
The Dubious Miss Dalrymple, 1990
The Anonymous Miss Addams, 1989
The Playful Lady Penelope, 1988
The Questioning Miss Quinton, 1987
The Mischievous Miss Murphy, 1987
The Savage Miss Saxon, 1985
The Lurid Lady Lockport, 1984
The Rambunctious Lady Royston,
    1982
The Tenacious Miss Tamerlane, 1982
The Belligerent Miss Boynton, 1982

Category Novels Written as Kasey Michaels

Silhouette Romance

The Ravens Assignment, #1613, 2002
Raffling Ryan, #1481, 2000
Jessie's Expecting, #1475, 2000
Marrying Maddy, #1469, 2000
The Dad Next Door, #1108, 1995
Timely Matrimony, #1030, 1994
Marriage in a Suitcase, #949, 1993
Uncle Daddy, #916, 1993
Prenuptial Agreement, #898, 1992

Sydney's Folly, #834, 1991
Lion on the Prowl, #808, 1991
Romeo in the Rain, #743, 1990
His Chariot Awaits, #701, 1990
To Marry at Christmas, #616, 1988
Popcorn and Kisses, #572, 1988
Compliments of the Groom, #542,
    1987
Maggie's Miscellany, #331, 1984

Other Category Titles

A Bride After All, Silhouette Special Edition, #2047, 2010
Suddenly a Bride, Silhouette Special Edition, #2035, 2010
The Tycoon's Secret, Silhouette Desire #1910, 2008
Texas Sheikhs: His Innocent Temptress, Harlequin American Romance # 869,
    2001
The Hopechest Bride, Silhouette: The Coltons #12, 2001
Beloved Wolf, Silhouette: The Coltons #1, 2001
Five's a Crowd, Harlequin Love & Laughter #3, 1996
Husbands Don't Grow on Trees, Silhouette Truly Yours #8, 1995

Novels Written as Michelle Kasey

The Somerville Farce, 1991
The Difficult Disguise, 1990

Moonlight Masquerade, 1989
The Enterprising Lord Edward, 1989
The Ruthless Lord Rule, 1987
The Toplofty Lord Thorpe, 1986
The Beleaguered Lord Bourne, 1985

Other Works

With Kathryn Seidick

Or You Can Let Him Go, 1984

Research Sources

Encyclopedias and Handbooks

"Kasey Michaels." *Literature Resource Center.* (subscription database). 2009.
    http://galenet.galegroup.com/. Last visited July 2009.

Biographies and Interviews

Coleman, Sandy. "Writer's Corner for October 2005: Kasey Michaels. *All About
    Romance.* October 2005. http://www.likesbooks.com/kaseymichaels.
    html. Last viewed July 2009.
"Come Get to Know: Kasey Michaels." *Mystery Lovers Corner.* http://www.
    sleuthedit.com/KaseyMichaels/Interview.html. Last visited July 2009.
White, Claire E. "A Conversation with Kasey Michaels. *The Internet Writ-
    ing Journal.* http://www.internetwritingjournal.com/mar06/michaels.htm.
    Last viewed July 2009.

Web Site

Kasey Michaels. http://www.kaseymichaels.com/. Last visited December
    2009. Kasey Michaels official Web site; includes links to her backlist,
    biographical information, awards, and excerpts from her newest titles.

Linda Lael Miller (1949–)

Western / Contemporary / Paranormal / Historical / Category

Biographical Sketch

Miller was born in eastern Washington state and her father was the Marshall
of their small town. Her love of the American West and the Western novel in
particular was fostered by her upbringing.

While westerns are the genre most associated with Miller, she also has written successful vampire and time-travel novels. Miller's heroines are strong women, able to stand on their own but also wanting to be loved, while her heroes follow the model of the dominant male who is strong when the time and the situation demand it. Miller's more recent releases have downplayed the sensuality of her earlier works.

Being a successful writer has allowed Miller the opportunity to travel the world. In addition to writing and traveling, Miller has set up a successful scholarship program that assists women over 25 in pursuing their education. In 2007, Miller received the Romance Writers of America Lifetime Achievement Award.

Maybe she wasn't such a bad mother, after all. Okay she wasn't exactly rising out of the ashes of her life, phoenix-like, not just yet anyway, but she could see a glimmer of light, faint, as a distant star, through the wreckage. There was reason to hope.

Linda Lael Miller
Last Chance Cafe, 2002

Major Works

Novels in Series

Montana Creeds

A Creed Country Christmas, 2009
Montana Creeds: Tyler, 2009
Montana Creeds: Dylan, 2009
Montana Creeds: Logan, 2009

MoJo Books

Deadly Deceptions, 2008
Deadly Gamble, 2006

Stone Creek

At Home in Stone Creek, Silhouette Special Edition #2205, 2009
The Bridegroom, 2009
The Rustler, 2009
A Stone Creek Christmas, Silhouette Special Edition #1939, 2008
A Wanted Man, 2007
The Man From Stone Creek, 2006

Look Books

One Last Look, 2006
Never Look Back, 2004
Don't Look Now, 2003

McKettrick Family

McKettricks of Texas: Austin, 2010
McKettricks of Texas: Garrett, 2010
McKettricks of Texas: Tate, 2010
A McKettrick Christmas, 2009
The McKettrick Way, Silhouette Special Edition #1867, 2007
McKettrick's Heart, 2007
McKettrick's Pride, 2007

McKettrick's Luck, 2007
Sierra's Homecoming, Silhouette Special Edition #1795, 2006
McKettrick's Choice, 2005
Secondhand Bride, 2004
Shotgun Bride, 2003
High Country Bride, 2002

The Women of Primrose Creek

Megan, 2000
Skye, 2000
Christy, 2000
Bridget, 2000

Springwater Seasons

Springwater Wedding, 2001
A Springwater Christmas, 1999
Jessica, 1999
Miranda, 1999
Savannah, 1999
Rachel, 1999
Springwater, 1999

Vampire Series

Tonight and Always, 1996
Time Without End, 1995
For All Eternity, 1994
Forever and the Night, 1993

Quaid Series

Princess Annie, 1994
Taming Charlotte, 1993
Yankee Wife, 1993

Orphan Train

Caroline and the Raider, 1992
Emma and the Outlaw, 1991
Lily and the Major, 1990

Australian Book Series

Angelfire, 1989
Moonfire, 1988

Novels

Last Chance Café, 2002
Courting Susanna, 2000
One Wish, 2000
Two Brothers: The Gunslinger &
    The Lawman, 1998
The Vow, 1998
My Outlaw, 1997
Together, 1996

Knights, 1996
Pirates, 1995
The Legacy, 1994
Daniel's Bride, 1992
My Darling Melissa, 1990
Wanton Angel, 1987
Lauralee, 1986

Category Novels

Silhouette Special Edition

Here and Then, #762, 1992
There and Now, #754, 1992
Ragged Rainbows, #324, 1986
State Secrets, #277, 1985

Silhouette Desire

Wild About Harry, #667, 1991
Glory, Glory, #607, 1990
Escape from Cabriz, #589, 1990
Mixed Messages, #568, 1990
Daring Moves, #547, 1990
Just Kate, #516, 1989
Only Forever, #480, 1989
Used-To-Be Lovers, #438, 1988

Silhouette Intimate Moments

Part of the Bargain, #87, 1985
Snowflakes on the Sea, #59, 1984

Tapestry

Memory's Embrace, #80, 1986
Corbin's Fancy, #69, 1985
Willow, #51, 1984
Banner O'Brien, #44, 1984
Desire and Destiny, #30, 1983
Fletcher's Woman, #22, 1983

Research Sources

Encyclopedias and Handbooks

Kemp, Barbara. "Linda Lael Miller." In *Twentieth-Century Romance and Historical Writers.* Ed. Aruna Vasudevan. 3rd ed. London: St. James Press. 1990. pp. 457–458.

"Linda Lael Miller." *Literature Resource Center.* (subscription database). 2008. http://galenet.galegroup.com/. Last visited June 2009.

Mosley, Shelley and van Winkle, Sandra. "Linda Lael Miller." In *Romance Today: An A-To-Z Guide to Contemporary American Romance Writers.* Ed. John Charles and Shelley Mosley. Westport, CT: Greenwood. 2007. pp. 274–278.

Biographies and Interviews

"ARR Interview with Linda Lael Miller." *A Romance Review.* April 2002. http://www.aromancereview.com/interviews/lindalaelmiller.phtml. Last visited September 2009.

Bexte, Martina. "Linda Lael Miller Comes Full Circle in Life and in Storytelling." *Bookloons.* July 2006. http://bookloons.com/cgi-bin/Columns. asp?name=Linda%20Lael%20Miller&type=Interview. Last visited September 2009.

Cooley, Holly. "Spotlight on Romance: The Booklist Interview: Linda Lael Miller." *The Booklist,* Volume 96, Issue 2, September 15, 1999. p 243.

Jaegly, Peggy. "Linda Lael Miller." *Romantic Hearts: A Personal Reference for Romance Readers.* 3rd ed. Lanham, MD: Scarecrow Press. 1997. pp. 88–89.

Kayle, Hillary S. "Linda Lael Miller: A Vivid Childhood Imagination." *Publisher's Weekly,* Volume 247, Issue 28, July 10, 2000. p. 28.

"'Step Up and Speak': An Interview with Linda Lael Miller." *The Humane Society of the United States.* January 18, 2007. http://www.hsus.org/pets/ pets_related_news_and_events/step_up_and_speak.html. Last visited September 2009.

Webster, Dan. "Author's Perseverance Leads to Storybook Career." *Knight Ridder Tribune Business News.* February 10, 2007.

Criticism and Readers' Guides

Santaularia, Isabel. "The Fallacy of Eternal Love: Romance, Vampires and Love in Linda Lael Miller's *Forever and the Night* and *For All Eternity.*" In *The Aesthetics of Ageing: Critical Approaches to Literary Representations of the Ageing Process.* Ed. Maria O'Neill, Carmen Llena Zamorano, and Brian J. Worsfold. Lerida, Spain: Universitat de Lleida. 2002. pp. 111–126.

Web Site

Linda Lael Miller. http://www.lindalaelmiller.com/. Last visited December 2009. The offical Web site for Linda Lael Miller; includes a biography, a complete backlist of titles, a list of her awards, and information on her personal appearances.

Susan Elizabeth Phillips

Contemporary / Historical

Biographical Sketch

Susan Elizabeth Phillips was born in Ohio and attended Ohio University, graduating with a bachelor of fine arts. On a whim, she began writing with a friend who loved reading as much as she did. After completing half of the manuscript, they submitted the unfinished work and a publisher bought it. Phillips's friend moved out of the area, but Phillips had fallen in love with writing, and continued on. Phillips now lives in the Chicago area with her husband and two grown sons.

Phillips's stories are known for their humor and her heroines are intelligent but can be eccentric. Her heroes, although, not the dominant males of earlier romance novels, do have strong dominant characteristics. In 2006, Phillips received the Romance Writers of America Lifetime Achievement Award and is a member of the RWA Hall of Fame.

All the blood rushed from her head. The strobes fired, the cameras snapped, the back of her hand flew to her mouth. After so many months of holding it together, she lost her way, and her eyes flooded with tears.

Susan Elizabeth Phillips
What I Did For Love, 2009

Major Works

Novels in Series

Chicago Stars

Natural Born Charmer, 2008
Match Me If You Can, 2005
This Heart of Mine, 2001
Dream a Little Dream, 1998
Nobody's Baby But Mine, 1997
Heaven, Texas, 1995
It Had to Be You, 1994

Bonner Family

Dream a Little Dream, 1998
Nobody's Baby But Mine, 1997

Wynette, Texas Books

What I Did for Love, 2009

Lady Be Good, 1999
Fancy Pants, 1989

Novels

Ain't She Sweet, 2004
Breathing Room, 2003
Just Imagine, 2001(originally published as *Risen Glory*)
First Lady, 2000
Kiss an Angel, 1996
Honey Moon, 1993
Hot Shot, 1991
Glitter Baby, 1987
Risen Glory, 1984

Collaborations

With Claire Kiehl

The Copeland Bride, 1983 (written as Justine Cole)

Other Works

"Susan Elizabeth Phillips." *Romantic Hearts: A Personal Reference for Romance Readers.* Ed. Peggy J. Jaegly. 3rd ed. Lanham, MD: Scarecrow Press. 1997. pp. 106–107.

"Romance and the Empowerment of Women." In *Dangerous Men and Adventurous Women: Romance Writers on the Appeal of the Romance.* Ed. Jayne Ann Krentz. Philadelphia: University of Pennsylvania Press. 1992. pp. 65–73.

Research Sources

Encyclopedias and Handbooks

Charles, John, Mosley, Shelly, Hamilton-Selway, Joanne, and van Winkle, Sandra. "Susan Elizabeth Phillips." In *Romance Today: An A-To-Z Guide to Contemporary American Romance Writers.* Ed. John Charles and Shelley Mosley. Westport, CT: Greenwood. 2007. pp. 296–300.

"Susan Elizabeth Phillips." *Literature Resource Center.* (subscription database). 2008. http://galenet.galegroup.com/. Last visited June 2009.

Biographies and Interviews

"Author Susan Elizabeth Phillips on The Chicago Stars Series." *Romantic Times Book Reviews Presents video interview.* http://www.youtube.com/watch?v=tNzsS14Yl5c&feature=related. Last visited September 2009.

Harper, Karen. "Susan Elizabeth Phillips." *Ohioana Quarterly.* Summer 2009. http://www.ohioana.org/quarterly/summer2009/phillips.pdf. Last visited September 2009.

Huseby, Sandy. "This Heart of Mine: Interview by Sandy Huseby." *Book Page.* February 2001. http://www.bookpage.com/books-8211-This+Heart+of+Mine. Last visited September 2009.

"Some Time with Susan Elizabeth Phillips." *All About Romance.* 1997. http://www.likesbooks.com/int3.html. Last visited September 2009.

Weiss, Angela. "Interview with Susan Elizabeth Phillips." *Die Romantische Bucherecke.* http://www.die-buecherecke.de/sep2.htm. Last visited September 2009.

Web Site

Susan Elizabeth Phillips. http://susanelizabethphillips.com/. Last visited December 2009. The official Web site for Susan Elizabeth Phillips; includes a message board for readers, a newsletter, a complete backlist of titles, and a link to personal appearances.

If You Like Susan Elizabeth Phillips

Humor is always a key element in any Phillips novel, and she writes entertaining, fun stories. The fact that Phillips's heroines aren't perfect makes them all the more human and easier to identify with. In turn, her heroes, many of whom are professional athletes, are strong enough to not only know what they want but to do what they need to get it.

You May Like

Jennifer Crusie

Jennifer Crusie writes witty, entertaining love stories that feature the support of family or family of choice. The heroines are not perfect and are occasionally required to solve problems not of their making. The heroes are smart, strong, and are willing to work for the love of the heroine. Crusie's stories revolve around friendships, family, and love in a very entertaining (snarky) way.

Cathie Linz

Cathie Linz writes entertaining, contemporary stories. Her heroines are often unconventional for romance novels, and the heroes are smart men who are smart enough to love an unconventional woman. No overly emotional struggles or serial killers are found in a Linz story.

Kasey Michaels

Kasey Michaels writes historical and contemporary romances that are laugh-out-loud funny. Her contemporary stories feature heroines who know there is more to life than the lives they are living. The heroes are smart, fun, and occasionally outrageous, as in the Maggie Kelly series.

Julia Quinn

While Quinn writes historical novels, her tone and use of humor is similar to that of Phillips. Quinn's stories take place among the *ton,* the aristocracy of the time, and her characters thrive in that arena. However, Quinn's stories are without most of the emotional angst found in some historical novels, and the heroes display a more sensitive nature than a traditional dominant male.

Mary Jo Putney / M. J. Putney (1946–)

Historical / Regency / Contemporary / Paranormal

Biographical Sketch

An avid reader all her life, Mary Jo Putney was born in upstate New York and graduated from Syracuse University with degrees in 18th-century British literature and industrial design. Putney worked in London and then moved to California to start her own graphic design business. After purchasing a computer for her office, Putney realized that she could begin writing novels, a long-held dream. Her first effort was purchased, and she continued from there. Putney, currently, lives in the Baltimore area of Maryland.

Putney's novels are not of the light and fluffy Regency variety, instead her historical and contemporary novels are emotional and angst-ridden. Characters die, and the Napoleonic war is represented as dangerous and unpleasant rather than a great triumph. Putney's heroines are strong women of necessity who face crisis with competence and practicality and rarely are they the standard just-out-of-the-school-room Miss of most historical novels. In turn, her heroes are strong men who have often been, misjudged by their society.

> *"Your sangfroid is legendary, but even so, the reports do you less than justice.*
> *If the devil himself walked in, I think you would ask him if he played whist."*
> *"Never play whist with the devil, my dear. He cheats."*

Mary Jo Putney
The Bargain, 1999

Major Works

Novels in Series

Lost Lords Series

Never Less Than a Lady, 2010
Loving a Lost Lord, 2009

Guardian Series

A Distant Magic, 2007
Stolen Magic, 2005
A Kiss of Fate, 2004

Circle of Friends

Twist of Fate, 2003
The Spiral Path, 2002
The Burning Point, 2000

Bride Trilogy

The Bartered Bride, 2002
The China Bride, 2000
The Wild Child, 1999

The Fallen Angels

One Perfect Rose, 1997
River of Fire, 1996
Shattered Rainbows, 1996
Angel Rogue (revised from *The Rogue* and *the Runaway*), 1995
Dancing in the Wind, 1994
Petals in the Storm (Revised from *The Controversial Countess*), 1993
Thunder and Roses, 1993

The Silk Trilogy

Veils of Silk, 1992
Silk and Secrets, 1992
Silk and Shadows, 1991

Novels

The Marriage Spell, 2006
The Bargain (revised from *The Would-Be Widow*), 1999
The Rake (revised from *The Rake and the Reformer*), 1998
Uncommon Vows, 1991
Dearly Beloved, 1990

The Rogue and the Runaway, 1990
Carousel of Hearts, 1989
The Controversial Countess, 1989
The Rake and the Reformer, 1989
The Would-Be Widow, 1988
Lady of Fortune, 1988
The Diabolical Baron, 1987

Other Works

"The Writer's Journey: Like a Lemming over a Cliff." In *North American Romance Writers.* Ed. Kay Mussell and Johanna Tunon. London: Scarecrow Press. 1999. pp. 159–166.

"Mary Jo Putney." *Romantic Hearts: A Personal Reference for Romance Readers.* 3rd ed. Ed. Peggy Jaegly. Lanham, MD: Scarecrow Press. 1997. pp. 110–111.

"Welcome to the Dark Side." *Dangerous Men and Adventurous Women: Romance Writers on the Appeal of the Romance.* Ed. Jayne Ann Krentz. Philadelphia: University of Pennsylvania Press. 1992. pp. 121–130.

Research Sources

Encyclopedias and Handbooks

Charles, John. "Mary Jo Putney." In *Romance Today: An A-To-Z Guide to Contemporary American Romance Writers.* Ed. John Charles and Shelley Mosley. Westport, CT: Greenwood. 2007. pp. 305–308.
"Mary Jo Putney." *Literature Resource Center.* (subscription database). 2008. http://galenet.galegroup.com/. Last visited June 2009.

Biographies and Interviews

"At the Back Fence: The Burning Point." *Laurie Likes Books.* May 15, 2000. http://www.likesbooks.com/95.html#putney. Last visited September 2009.
Jorgenson, Jane. "Writer's Corner: Mary Jo Putney: A Look Back and a Look Ahead." *All About Romance.* June 2004. http://www.likesbooks. com/putney.html. Last visited September 2009.
"Mary Jo Putney: Trial by Romance." *Crescent Blues.* http://www.crescent blues.com/4_4issue/int_mary_jo_putney.shtml. Last visited September 2009.
White, Claire E. "A Conversation with Mary Jo Putney." *Writer's Write.* November/December 2004. http://www.writerswrite.com/journal/dec04/ putney.htm. Last visited September 2009.
Williams, Juan. "Interview: Two Romance Novelists Define and Defend the Genre." *Talk of the Nation.* National Public Radio. July 24, 2000. http:// www.npr.org/templates/story/story.php?storyId=1079867. Last visited January 2010.

Criticism and Readers' Guides

McCay, Mary A. "Love's Labors Won: Romance Fiction and the Politics of Love." *New Orleans Review,* Volume 27, Issue 1, 2001. pp. 171–183.
Seale, Maura. " 'I Find Some Hindu Practices Like Burning Widows, Utterly Bizarre.': Representations of Sati and Questions of Choice." In *Veils of Silk." Empowerment Versus Oppression: Twenty First Century Views of Popular Romance Novels.* Ed. Sally Goade. Newcastle Upon Tyne, England: Cambridge Scholars. 2007. pp. 129–147.

Web Sites

Mary Jo Putney. http://www.maryjoputney.com/. Last visited December 2009. The official Web site of Mary Jo Putney; includes a complete backlist, biographical information, links for writers, and a calendar of events.

Word Wenches. http://wordwenches.typepad.com/word_wenches/. Last visited December 2009. A multi-author blog, featuring Mary Jo Putney.

If You Like Mary Jo Putney

Mary Jo Putney writes an emotional story like no other. Her historical novels, especially the *Fallen Angels,* pull the reader into the time period through her richly layered characters. Putney has researched the Napoleonic wars extensively and effectively uses that as a backdrop.

You May Like

Mary Balogh

Mary Balogh writes character-driven Regency and historical romances. Her books follow closely along the Jane Austen and Georgette Heyer style of historical novel focusing on marriage and accidentally finding love. Frequently characters can be found in several books, with minor characters in one novel becoming the hero or heroine in a subsequent novel.

Loretta Chase

Loretta Chase writes Regency- and Victorian-era stories that are rigorously researched. Her heroes are damaged emotionally and feel they cannot love. Her heroines are strong women who find love is worth the risk. Chase's stories are always entertaining.

Candice Hern

Candice Hern writes beautifully crafted Regency novels with authentic plots and characters. Hern's multiple series allow the reader to revisit old characters in the new stories. If you can find Hern's early Signet Regencies in a used bookstore, you will have found some truly enjoyable Regency novels.

Judith Ivory

Ivory's fast-paced and entertaining stories take place during the Victorian era. Her unconventional heroines, working women, courtesans, or older than the schoolroom Miss match the heroes in strength and disregard for societal norms.

Stephanie Laurens

Laurens's stories are character-driven and feature alpha male heroes, and heroines who are confident enough to stand up to them. While the stories take place during the Regency time period and can be emotionally driven, they are not stuffy. The stories are all very sensual and can be humorous.

Julia Quinn (1970–)

Regency / Historical

Biographical Sketch

Julia Quinn is the pseudonym of Julie Pottinger. After graduating from Harvard University and preparing to go to medical school, Quinn began writing romance novels. Her first work sold and Quinn continued to write romance novels while working on the prerequisite classes for medical school. Finally Quinn realized that writing was what she really wanted to do after starting at Yale Medical School. After spending several years on the East Coast, Quinn and her husband now live in the Seattle area.

Quinn's stories are entertaining Regency stories that are mostly written in series, allowing readers to revisit characters from previous stories. Quinn's heroines are spunky, confident, and smart who live by the structure imposed by the aristocracy of the *ton,* without being oppressed by it. The heroes are strong, sensitive, and appreciative of the heroines for who they are, rather than for their titles or dowries.

> *Eloise just stared at him. As long as she lived, she'd never understand men. She had four brothers, and quite frankly should have understood them better than most women, and maybe it had taken all of her twenty-eight years to come to this realization, but men were, quite simply, freaks.*

Julia Quinn
To Sir Phillip with Love, 2003

Major Works

Novels in Series

Bevelstoke / Valentine Families

What Happens in London, 2009
The Secret Diaries of Miss Miranda Cheever, 2007

Wyndham Family

Mr. Cavendish, I Presume, 2008
The Lost Duke of Wyndham, 2008

Bridgerton Family

On the Way to the Wedding, 2006
It's in His Kiss, 2005
When He Was Wicked, 2004
To Sir Phillip, With Love, 2003
Romancing Mr. Bridgerton, 2002

An Offer from a Gentleman, 2001
The Viscount Who Loved Me, 2000
The Duke and I, 2000

Lyndon Sisters

Brighter than the Sun, 1997
Everything and the Moon, 1997

Splendid Trilogy

Minx, 1996
Dancing at Midnight, 1995
Splendid, 1995

Novels

Ten Things I Love About You, 2010
How to Marry a Marquis, 1999
To Catch an Heiress, 1998

Other Works

"Laurie's News & Views Issue 42: Julia Quinn Guests." *All About Romance.* December 20, 1997. http://www.likesbooks.com/42.htm. Last visited September 2009.

Research Sources

Encyclopedias and Handbooks

"Julia Quinn." *Literature Resource Center.* (subscription database). 2005. http://galenet.galegroup.com/. Last visited June 2009.

Biographies and Interviews

Albers, Lisa. "Romancing the Tome." *Seattle Woman Magazine.* February 2008. http://www.seattlewomanmagazine.com/articles/feb08–2.htm. Last visited September 2009.
Coleman, Sandy. "Writer's Corner: Julia Quinn." *All About Romance.* June 2005. http://www.likesbooks.com/juliaquinn2005.html. Last visited September 2009.
Gaston, Diane. "Interview with Julia Quinn." *Risky Regencies.* October 27, 2008. http://riskyregencies.blogspot.com/2008/10/interview-with-julia-quinn.html. Last visited September 2009.
Grossman, Lev. "Rewriting the Romance. *Time,* Volume 161, Issue 5, February 3, 2003. p. 64.
Hern, Candice. "Interview." *Dishing with Divas,* available on Julia Quinn's Web site. June 12, 2006. http://www.juliaquinn.com/bonus-features/blog.htm#08oct27. Last visited September 2009.

"Julia Quinn Makes Her Own Destiny." *All About Romance.* 1996. http://www.likesbooks.com/quinn.html. Last visited September 2009.

Rich, Haven. "And the Mystery Author Is..." *Romantic Inks.* December 2, 2006. http://romanticinks.com/2006/12/02/and-the-mystery-author-is/. Last visited September 2009.

Wehr, Isolde and L. Pia. "Interview with Julia Quinn." *Die Romantische Bucherecke.* February 2001. http://www.die-buecherecke.de/quinn2.htm. Last visited September 2009.

Wisconsin Public Radio. "The Food of Love." *To the Best of Our Knowledge.* 2002. http://www.wpr.org/book/020210b.htm. Last visited September 2009.

Yamashita, Brianna. "The Strongest Link: Talks with Julia Quinn." *Publisher's Weekly,* Volume 250, Issue 19, May 12, 2003. p. 50.

Web Site

Julia Quinn Romance Author. http://www.juliaquinn.com/. Last visited December 2009. Julia Quinn's official Web site; includes a biography, a list of titles, an FAQ, and information about her personal appearances.

The Bulletin Board of Eloisa James and Julia Quinn. http://eloisajames.net/board/. Last visited December 2009. A discussion board for fans of James and Quinn to discuss their books.

If You Like Julia Quinn

Quinn's stories are humorous and entertaining, and because most are part of a series, allow the reader to revisit previous characters. Her stories take place among the *ton* and her characters thrive in that arena. However, Quinn's stories are without most of the emotional angst found in some historical romances and the heroes display a more sensitive nature than a traditional dominant male.

You May Like

Jo Beverley

Jo Beverley writes mostly series novels, such as her Malloren series, which focuses on the fates of the brothers and sisters of the Malloren family. Her titles cover the Georgian and Regency time periods and feature strong women, and men who like strong women whether they know it or not. In 2000 her novel *Devilish,* produced one of the most anticipated heroes of the 21st century in the Marquess of Rothgar.

Loretta Chase

Loretta Chase writes Regency- and Victorian-era stories that are rigorously researched. Her heroes are damaged emotionally and feel they cannot love. Her heroines are strong women who find love is worth the risk. Chase's stories are always entertaining.

Lisa Kleypas

Kleypas is known for strong romantic characters in the Regency setting. Although the Regency genre is known for its focus on members of the *ton* and the aristocracy, Kleypas's historicals feature characters that revolve around the *ton* but not of the aristocracy itself. Her 1994 novel *Dreaming of You* is a wonderful example of Regency life built around the aristocracy.

Jayne Anne Krentz Writing as Amanda Quick

Amanda Quick's Regency stories, like many of Krentz's stories, contain both a mystery and paranormal elements. One example is Quick's Arcane Society series, which features strong, scientifically focused heroes, and heroines who are strong and smart enough to keep up with the hero intellectually.

Stephanie Laurens

Laurens's stories are character-driven and feature dominant male heroes, and heroines who are confident enough to stand up to them. While the stories take place during the Regency time period and can be emotional, they are not stuffy. Laurens's stories are all very sensual and can be humorous.

Nora Roberts / J. D. Robb (1950–)

Contemporary / Romantic Suspense / Paranormal

Biographical Sketch

Nora Roberts began writing when she was stranded in her house with two small children during a weeklong snow storm, in order to alleviate the boredom, but she continued to write even after the snowstorm. Roberts attended Catholic school as a child and attributes her work ethic as a writer to her upbringing. In 1985, Roberts married her second husband, Bruce Wilder, who now owns a bookstore in western Maryland where Roberts lives.

Roberts's prolific output has not affected the quality of her work. Her heroines are competent women who will risk their hearts for the men they love while the heroes are strong men, but not the overbearing males of the 1980s. The love and support of family and friends are strong elements featured in most of Roberts's novels.

In 1997 Nora Roberts discovered that several of her novels were plagiarized by fellow romance author Janet Dailey. The lawsuit was settled out of court and Roberts donated the settlement to literacy charities. In 1997 Nora Roberts received the Lifetime Achievement Award from the Romance Writers of America and is a member of the Romance Writers of America Hall of Fame. The RWA Lifetime Achievement Award was renamed the Nora Roberts Lifetime Achievement Award in 2008.

> *In cottages and pubs, people gathered around fires and talked of their farms and their roofs, the loved ones who had emigrated to Germany or the States. It hardly mattered whether they had left the day before, or a generation. Ireland was losing its people, as it had all but lost its language.*

Nora Roberts
Born in Ice, 1995

Major Works

Novels in Series Written as Nora Roberts

Bride Quartet

Savor the Moment, 2010
Bed of Roses, 2009
Vision in White, 2009

Sign of Seven

The Pagan Stone, 2008
The Hollow, 2008
Blood Brothers, 2007

Circle Trilogy

Valley of Silence, 2006
Dance of the Gods, 2006
Morrigan's Cross, 2006

In the Garden Trilogy

Red Lily, 2005
Black Rose, 2005
Blue Dahlia, 2004

Key Trilogy

Key of Valor, 2004
Key of Knowledge, 2003
Key of Light, 2003

Three Sisters Island Trilogy

Face the Fire, 2002
Heaven and Earth, 2001
Dance upon the Air, 2001

The Irish Trilogy

Heart of the Sea, 2000
Tears of the Moon, 2000
Jewels of the Sun, 1999

Chesapeake Bay

Chesapeake Blue, 2002
Inner Harbor, 1999
Rising Tides, 1998
Sea Swept, 1998

Dream Trilogy

Finding the Dream, 1997
Holding the Dream, 1997
Daring to Dream, 1996

Concannon Sisters or Born In Trilogy

Born in Shame, 1996
Born in Ice, 1995
Born in Fire, 1994

Novels Written as Nora Roberts

The Search, 2010
Black Hills, 2009
Tribute, 2008
High Noon, 2007
Angels Fall, 2006
Blue Smoke, 2005
Northern Lights, 2004

Birthright, 2003
Remember When, 2003
Once Upon Midnight, 2003
Three Fates, 2002
Midnight Bayou, 2001
The Villa, 2001
Carolina Moon, 2000

River's End, 1999
The Reef, 1998
Homeport, 1998
Sanctuary, 1997
Montana Sky, 1996
True Betrayals, 1995
Hidden Riches, 1994
Private Scandals, 1993
Divine Evil, 1992

Carnal Innocence, 1992
Genuine Lies, 1991
Public Secrets, 1990
Sweet Revenge, 1989
Brazen Virtue, 1988
Sacred Sins, 1987
Hot Ice, 1987
Promise Me Tomorrow, 1984

Category Novels Written by Nora Roberts

Silhouette Intimate Moments

Night Shield, #1027, 2000
Enchanted Star, #835, 1998
Captive Star, #823, 1997
Hidden Star, #811, 1997
Megan's Mate, #745, 1996
The Heart of Devin MacKade, #697, 1996
The Return of Rafe MacKade, #631, 1995
Night Smoke, #595, 1994
Nightshade, #529, 1993
Unfinished Business, #433, 1992
Suzanna's Surrender, #397, 1991
Night Shadows, #373, 1991
Night Shift, #365, 1991
Times Change, #317, 1990
Time Was, #313, 1989
Gabriel's Angel, #300, 1989
Name of the Game, #264, 1988

Irish Rose, #232, 1988
The Playboy Prince, #212, 1987
Command Performance, #198, 1987
Mind Over Matter, #185, 1987
Risky Business, #160, 1986
Treasures Lost, Treasures Found, #150, 1986
Affaire Royale, #142, 1986
Art of Deception, #131, 1986
Duel Image, #123, 1985
Boundary Lines, #114, 1985
Partners, #94, 1985
The Right Path, #85, 1985
Rules of the Game, #70, 1984
A Matter of Choice, #49, 1984
Endings and Beginnings, #33, 1984
This Magic Moment, #25, 1983
Tonight and Always, #12, 1983
Once More with Feeling, #2, 1983

Silhouette Special Edition

Cordina's Crown Jewel, #1448, 2002
Considering Kate, #1379, 2001
Irish Rebel, #1328, 2000
The Perfect Neighbor, #1232, 1999
The Winning Hand, #1202, 1998
Waiting for Nick, #1088, 1997
The Fall of Shane MacKade, #1022, 1996
The Pride of Jared MacKade, #1000, 1995
Convincing Alex, #872, 1994

Falling for Rachel, #810, 1993
Charmed, #780, 1992
Entranced, #774, 1992
Captivated, #768, 1992
Luring a Lady, #709, 1991
For the Love of Lilah, #685, 1991
Without a Trace, #625, 1990
Taming Natasha, #583, 1990
The Welcoming, #553, 1989
Loving Jack, #499, 1989
Skin Deep, #475, 1988

Dance to the Piper, #463, 1988
The Last Honest Woman, #451, 1988
Local Hero, #427, 1988
For Now, Forever, #361, 1987
A Will and a Way, #345, 1986
Lessons Learned, #318, 1986
One Summer, #306, 1986
Second Nature, #288, 1986
Summer Desserts, #271, 1985

One Man's Art, #259, 1985
All the Possibilities, #247, 1985
Tempting Fate, #235, 1985
Playing the Odds, #225, 1985
Opposites Attract, #199, 1984
The Law is a Lady, #175, 1984
First Impressions, #162, 1984
Dance of Dreams, #116, 1983
Reflections, #100, 1983
The Heart's Victory, #59, 1982

Silhouette Romance

Courting Catherine, #801, 1991
Temptation, #529, 1987
Less of a Stranger, #299, 1984
Sullivan's Woman, #280, 1984
Storm Warning, #274, 1984
Untamed, #252, 1983
Her Mother's Keeper, #215, 1983

From this Day, #199, 1983
Island of Flowers, #180, 1982
Search for Love, #163, 1982
Song of the West, #143, 1982
Blithe Image, #127, 1982
Irish Thoroughbred, #81, 1981

Other Category Novels Written as Nora Roberts

A Man for Amanda, Silhouette Desire #649, 1991
Lawless, Harlequin Historical #21, 1989
Rebellion, Harlequin Historical #4, 1988
Night Moves, Harlequin Intrigue #19, 1985

Novels Written as J. D. Robb

Kindred in Death, 2009
Promises in Death, 2009
Strangers in Death, 2009
Salvation in Death, 2008
Creation in Death, 2007
Innocent in Death, 2007
Born in Death, 2006
Survivor in Death, 2005
Origin in Death, 2005
Divided in Death, 2004
Visions in Death, 2004
Portrait in Death, 2003
Imitation in Death, 2003
Reunion in Death, 2002

Purity in Death, 2002
Betrayal in Death, 2001
Seduction in Death, 2001
Witness in Death, 2000
Judgment in Death, 2000
Conspiracy in Death, 1999
Loyalty in Death, 1999
Holiday in Death, 1998
Ceremony in Death, 1997
Vengeance in Death, 1997
Rapture in Death, 1996
Immortal in Death, 1996
Naked in Death, 1995
Glory in Death, 1995

Other Works

"The Romance of Writing." In *North American Romance Writers*. Ed. Kay Mussell and Johanna Tunon. London: Scarecrow Press. 1999. pp. 191–201.

Movies Based on the Novels of Nora Roberts

Carson, David, director. *Blue Smoke*, Lifetime Television movie. February 12, 2007. *Internet Movie Database*. http://www.imdb.com/title/tt0893397/. Last visited September 2009.

Coolidge, Martha, director. *Tribute*, Lifetime Television movie. April 11, 2009. Internet Movie Database, http://www.imdb.com/title/tt1343115/. Last visited September 2009.

Hemecker, Ralph, director. *Midnight Bayou*, Lifetime Television movie. March 28, 2009. Internet Movie Database, http://www.imdb.com/title/tt1320347/. Last visited September 2009.

Hemecker, Ralph, director. *Angles Fall*, Lifetime Television movie. January 29, 2007. Internet Movie Database, http://www.imdb.com/title/tt0869921/. Last visited September 2009.

Markle, Peter, director. *High Noon*, Lifetime Television movie. April 4, 2009. Internet Movie Database, http://www.imdb.com/title/tt1359554/. Last visited September 2009.

Robe, Mike, director. *Northern Lights*, Lifetime Television movie. March 21, 2009. Internet Movie Database, http://www.imdb.com/title/tt1363127/. Last visited September 2009.

Robe, Mike, director. *Montana Sky*, Lifetime Television movie. February 5, 2007. Internet Movie Database. http://www.imdb.com/title/tt0860467/ Last visited September 2009.

Shea, Katt, director. *Sanctuary*, Lifetime Television movie. February 28 2001. Internet Movie Database, http://www.imdb.com/title/tt0272289./ Last visited September 2009.

Tolkin, Stephen, director. *Carolina Moon*, Lifetime Television movie. February 19, 2007. Internet Movie Database, http://www.imdb.com/title/tt0840787/. Last visited September 2009.

Research Sources

Encyclopedias and Handbooks

Charles, John, Mosley, Shelley and van Winkle, Sandra. "Nora Roberts." In *Romance Today: An A-To-Z Guide to Contemporary American Romance Writers*. Ed. John Charles and Shelley Mosley. Westport, CT: Greenwood. 2007. pp. 329–334.

Kemp, Barbara. "Nora Roberts." In *Twentieth-Century Romance and Historical Writers*. Ed. Aruna Vasudevan. 3rd ed. London: St. James Press. 1990. pp. 562–563.

"Nora Roberts." *Literature Resource Center.* (subscription database). 2009. http://galenet.galegroup.com/. Last visited June 2009.

Biographies and Interviews

Brogan Struckel, Katie. "Nora Roberts." *Writer's Digest.* February 11, 2008. http://www.writersdigest.com/article/Nora_Roberts/. Last visited December 2009.

Burke, Jan. "Success in Death: An Interview with Nora Roberts aka J. D. Robb." *Mystery Scene,* Volume 83, Winter 2004. pp. 16–21.

Danehy-Oakes, Dan'l. "The Mystery of Nongenre SF: The Case of Nora Roberts." *New York Review of Science Fiction,* Volume 13, Number 10, June 2001. pp. 12–14.

Mowery, Linda. "Nora Roberts on Her MacGregor Series." *All About Romance.* September 22, 1997. http://www.likesbooks.com/roberts.html. Last visited September 2009.

Mussell, Kay. "Paradoxa Interview with Nora Roberts." *Paradoxa,* Volume 3, Issue 1/2, 1997. pp. 155–163.

Quinn, Judy. "Nora Roberts: A Celebration of Emotions." *Publisher's Weekly,* Volume 245, Issue 8, February 23, 1998. pp. 46–47.

Simon, Scott. "A Love Affair with the Romance Novel." *Weekend Edition Saturday.* National Public Radio. July 18, 2009. http://www.npr.org/templates/story/story.php?storyId=106770512. Last visited September 2009.

St. John, Cheryl. "Nora Roberts Interview." *From the Heart . . . Cheryl St. John.* December 26, 2007. http://cherylstjohn.blogspot.com/2007/12/nora-roberts-interview.html. Last visited September 2009.

"10 Questions for Nora Roberts." *Time.* November 29, 2007. http://www.time.com/time/magazine/article/0,9171,1689202,00.html. Last visited September 2009.

Titchener, Louise. "Drive, Discipline & Desire." *Writer's Digest,* Volume 77, Number 2, February 1997. pp. 25–27, 53.

Criticism and Readers' Guides

Little, Denise and Hayden Laura, Eds. *The Official Nora Roberts Companion.* New York: Berkeley. 2003.

Regis, Pamela. "Complicating Romances and Their Readers: Barrier and Point of Ritual Death in Nora Roberts' Category Fiction." *Paradoxa,* Volume 3, Issue 1/2, 1997, pp. 145–157.

Web Site

Nora Roberts. http://www.noraroberts.com/. Last visited December 2009. The official Web site of Nora Roberts; includes links to a backlist, biographical information, a message board for her fans to discuss her works, and a newsletter.

If You Like Nora Roberts

Roberts writes fast-paced, character-driven stories. Her heroines are competent women willing to take risks for love and her heroes are strong males who want to protect the women they love. Family is a strong feature in almost all of Roberts's works. While her earlier works are lighter, her more recent stories usually have a romantic suspense element.

You May Like

Suzanne Brockmann

Suzanne Brockmann writes action, adventure, and romantic suspense romance novels. Her stories feature military men of action who find love in unexpected places. In turn, her heroines are as tough as the heroes, with emotional scars much like those possessed by heroes in other romance novels. Fast-paced action and smart dialogue make a Brockman novel a fun read.

Jayne Anne Krentz

Krentz publishes novels in a number of genres under both her own name and her various pseudonyms. Regardless of genre, many of these novels contain both mystery and paranormal elements, along with strong heroes and smart heroines.

Elizabeth Lowell

Lowell writes the dominant male hero as rough and tough as the readers will allow. Her medieval and contemporary stories feature heroes who never thought of love and heroines who can convince the hero that love can exist.

Susan Elizabeth Phillips

Susan Elizabeth Phillips writes stories with often imperfect, struggling heroines and strong males who know what they want and work hard to get it. Humor and strong characters are always key elements in any Phillips novel.

Christina Skye

Skye's stories are complex and occasionally violent. The heroines may be unconventional with unique skills. The heroes are strong and protective even if they aren't sure about love. Skye's strength is the dialogue of the character-driven stories. In the Draycott Abbey series, a witty ghost adds humor and a touch of the paranormal.

Sharon Sala / Dinah McCall

Contemporary / Romantic Suspense / Category

Biographical Sketch

Sharon Sala began writing in the early 1980s but her two initial works never made it to a publisher. When her father and then her only sister died within months of each other in 1985, Sala decided that life was too short for regrets, and began writing again. In 1989, she finished the novel that would become *Sara's Angel* and sold it to a publisher on her first try. Sala writes under both her given name and the pseudonym Dinah McCall. She currently resides in Oklahoma and her rural background can be seen in many of her novels.

Sala's books fall in the romantic suspense subgenre and have a gritty reality that can seem to conflict with the down-home values and characters that populate her books. A belief in God is a core value with most of the characters. Most of the main characters in Sala's stories could be considered loners, who have at least temporarily found a place to settle down through hard work. While her books' locations may vary, there is always an element of small-town, strong neighbors, and a family-of-choice throughout the stories.

> *The defiance that had been with her for so long was gone. Losing the fury that came with the need for revenge has made room for his love. It seemed like a lifetime ago that he'd first seen her, carrying an unconscious man over her shoulder and out of a burning building.*

Sharon Sala
Bad Penny, 2008

Major Works

Novels in Series written by Sharon Sala

Cat Dupree

Bad Penny, 2008
Cut Throat, 2007
Nine Lives, 2006

Letty and Eulis

The Hen House, 2007
The Amen Trail, 2004
Whipporwill, 2003

Gambler's Daughters

Lucky, 1995
Queen, 1994
Diamond, 1994

Novels Written as Sharon Sala

Swept Aside, 2010
Torn Apart, 2010
Blown Away, 2010
The Warrior, 2009
The Healer, 2008
The Chosen, 2005
Missing, 2004
Out of the Dark, 2003
Dark Water, 2002
Reunion at Mossy Creek, 2002

Snowfall, 2001
Butterfly, 2000
Remember Me, 1999
Reunion, 1999
Sweet Baby, 1998
Finders Keepers, 1997
Second Chances, 1996
Deep in the Heart, 1996
Chance McCall, 1993

Silhouette Intimate Moments Titles Written as Sharon Sala

The Way to Yesterday, #1171, 2002
Familiar Strangers, #1082, 2001
Mission: Irresistible, #1016, 2000
A Place to Call Home, #973, 2000
Royal's Child, #913, 1999
Roman's Heart, #859, 1998

Ryder's Wife, #817, 1997
Shades of a Desperado, #757, 1997
When You Call My Name, #687,
   1996
The Miracle Man, #650, 1995
Annie and the Outlaw, #597, 1994

Other Category Titles Written as Sharon Sala

Aftershock, Silhouette Nocturne #49, 2008
Amber by Night, Silhouette Desire #1495, 2003
For Her Eyes Only, Silhouette 36 hours, 1997
Gentle Persuasion, Meteor/Kismet, 1993
Always a Lady, Meteor/Kismet, 1993
Honor's Promise, Meteor/Kismet, 1992
King's Ransom, Meteor/Kismet, 1992
Sara's Angel, Meteor/Kismet, 1991

Novels Written as Dinah McCall

The Survivors, 2007
Bloodlines, 2005
The Perfect Lie, 2003
Mimosa Grove, 2004
White Mountain, 2002
Storm Warning, 2001
The Return, 2000

Touchstone, 1999
Legend, 1998
Chase the Moon, 1997
Tallchief, 1997
Jackson Rule, 1996
Dreamcatcher, 1996

Research Sources

Encyclopedias and Handbooks

"Sharon Sala." *Literature Resource Center.* (subscription database). 2009.
   http://galenet.galegroup.com/. Last visited June 2009.

Biographies and Interviews

"ARR Interview with Sharon Sala." *A Romance Review.* November 2005. http://www.aromancereview.com/interviews/sharonsala.phtm. Last visited June 2009.

"Author Talk Interviews Sharon Sala." *Dear Author . . . Best Regards the Ja(y)nes.* May 30, 2008. http://dearauthor.com/wordpress/2008/05/30/author-talk-interviews-sharon-sala/. Last visited June 2009.

French, Liz. "I Will Survive: Sharon Sala and Her Alter Ego Dinah McCall Face Down the Terrible Twos." *Romantic Times,* Issue #277, 2007. p. 26.

Ketteringham, Kristin. "Sharon Sala—A Closer Look at the Successful Romance Author." *Associated Content: Arts & Entertainment.* September 24, 2007. http://www.associatedcontent.com/article/383487/sharon_sala_a_closer_look_at_the_successful.html. Last visited June 2009.

"Meet Sharon Sala "*Suspense Romance Writers.* http://suspenseromancewriters.com/authorinfo.cfm?authorID=444. Last visited June 2009.

Reymond, Ken. "Are You Playing By the Rules of Romance." *McClatchy-Tribune Business News.* February 14, 2007.

Web Site

Sharon Sala / Dinah McCall. http://www.sharonsalabooks.com/. Last visited December 2009. The official Web site for Sharon Sala; includes a biography, a backlist of her novels, a gallery of photos, and information for the media.

Christina Skye (1950–)

Contemporary / Romantic Suspense / Paranormal / Historical

Biographical Sketch

Christina Skye is the pseudonym used by Roberta Helmer Stalberg. She attended the University of Pennsylvania, receiving a bachelor's degree, and then attended the University of Ohio where she earned a master's and PhD degrees in Chinese literature. Skye spent several years in China working as a translator, and when she returned to the United States, she published several works about Chinese culture. After writing nonfiction for several years, Skye began to write fiction, and her first novel was published in 1990.

Skye's stories are complex and sometimes violent. The heroines are strong women—certainly not frail—with different abilities and skills, while her heroes are sensitive but strong, and will protect what they care for at all cost.

Clever dialogue between the main characters and the supporting characters provides additional depth and humor to the stories.

> *Paradise was fine when you were eighteen and crazy in love, enjoying a clothing-optional vacation. When you were working, paradise felt like salt scraping an old wound, reminding you of all that was wrong with your life.*

Christina Skye
Code Name: Blondie, 2006

Major Works

Novels in Series

Code Name

Code Name: Bikini, 2007
Code Name: Blondie, 2006
Code Name: Baby, 2005
Code Name: Princess, 2004
Code Name: Nanny, 2004

Draycott Abbey

Bound By Dreams, 2009
To Catch a Thief, 2008
The Perfect Gift, 1999
Christmas Knight, 1998
Season of Wishes, 1997

Key to Forever, 1997
Bride of the Mist, 1996
Bridge of Dreams, 1995
Draycott Legacy, 1995
Hour of the Rose, 1994

Novels

Hot Pursuit, 2003
My Spy, 2002
Going Overboard, 2001
2000 Kisses, 2000
Come the Dawn, 1995

Come the Night, 1994
East of Forever, 1993
The Ruby, 1992
The Black Rose, 1991
Defiant Captive, 1990

Other Works

Stalberg, Roberta Helmer. *Shopping in China: Arts, Crafts and the Unusual.* San Francisco: China Books & Periodicals. 1986.

Stalberg, Roberta Helmer and Nesi, Ruth. *China's Crafts: The Story of How They're Made and What They Mean.* London: Allen and Unwin. 1981.

Stalberg, Roberta Helmer. *The Poems of the Han-Shan Collection.* PhD Dissertation. The Ohio State University. 1977.

Research Sources

Encyclopedias and Handbooks

"Christina Skye." *Literature Resource Center.* (subscription database). 2008. http://galenet.galegroup.com/. Last visited June 2009.

Mosley, Shelley and van Winkle, Sandra. "Christina Skye." In *Romance Today: An A-To-Z Guide to Contemporary American Romance Writers.* Ed. John Charles and Shelley Mosley. Westport, CT: Greenwood. 2007. pp. 351–353.

Biographies and Interviews

"ARR Interview with Christina Skye." *A Romance Review.* June 2004. http://www.aromancereview.com/news/wmview.php?ArtCat=7&pos=100. Last visited September 2009.

Roark, John. "Love in the Afternoon: A Torrid Lunch with Two Romance Novelists Cooks Up Love in the Afternoon." *Phoenix New Times,* Volume 32, Issue 59, February 14, 2002. http://proquest.umi.com/. Last visited September 2009.

White, Claire E. "A Conversation with Christina Skye." *Writers Write.* January 2000. http://www.writerswrite.com/journal/jan00/skye.htm. Last visited September 2009.

Web Site

Christina Skye. http://www.christinaskye.com/. Last visited December 2009. The official Web site for Christina Skye; includes biographical information, a book list, photos, media information, and information about Skye's hobbies, Feng Shui and knitting.

Bertrice Small (1937–)

Historical / Paranormal / Contemporary

Biographical Sketch

Bertrice Small always wanted to be a writer, but since most women in the 1950s and 1960s held conventional jobs, Small attended secretarial school instead. In 1963, she met her husband, a historian. Once married, Small was free to write and in defiance of the current norms, ultimately, she became the worker in the family while her husband handled the domestic chores. She lives on Long Island, New York.

Small's stories are sensual, and her earlier works contain elements that have now been mostly dropped from the genre, specifically the rape of the heroine. Although, historical figures share the stage with her characters, historical facts remain accurate. Small's heroines are strong women who often take on the male roles of running the estate, business, and politics and many of her novels and series cover the entire life of the heroine, including not one hero, but many men who fill specific roles during specific time periods. Small's novel *Skye O'Malley* is considered a classic in the historical romance genre.

> *"I am going to turn you back in to the lady you were born to be, and then, dear girl, we shall go hunt for a nice young man who will not be frightened of you, and who shall love you and give you the sons and daughters this estate nurtures so well."*

Bertrice Small
Last Heiress, 2005

Major Works

Novels in Series

The World of Hetar

Crown of Destiny, 2010
The Sorceress of Belmair, 2008
The Twilight Lord, 2007
A Distant Tomorrow, 2006
Lara, 2005

The Border Chronicles

The Border Lord and the Lady, 2009
The Captive Heart, 2008
The Border Lord's Bride, 2007
A Dangerous Love, 2006

The Pleasures

Dangerous Pleasures, 2008
Sudden Pleasures, 2007
Forbidden Pleasures, 2006
Private Pleasures, 2004

The Friarsgate Inheritance

The Last Heiress, 2005
Phillippa, 2004
Until You, 2003
Rosamund, 2002

Skye's Legacy

Vixens, 2003
Just Beyond Tomorrow, 2002
Intrigued, 2001

Besieged, 2000
Bedazzled, 1999
Darling Jasmine, 1997

The O'Malley Saga

Wild Jasmine, 1992
Lost Love Found, 1989
This Heart of Mine, 1988
A Love for All Time, 1986
All the Sweet Tomorrows, 1984
Skye O'Malley, 1980

Novels

The Shadow Queen, 2009
The Dragon Lord's Daughters, 2004
The Duchess, 2001
A Memory of Love, 2000
The Innocent, 1999
Deceived, 1998
Betrayed, 1998
Hellion, 1996
The Love Slave, 1995
Love, Remember Me, 1994

To Love Again, 1993
A Moment in Time, 1991
The Spitfire, 1990
Blaze Wyndham, 1988
Enchantress Mine, 1987
Beloved, 1983
Unconquered, 1982
Adora, 1980
Love Wild and Fair, 1978
The Kadin, 1978

Research Sources

Encyclopedias and Handbooks

"Bertrice Small." *Literature Resource Center.* (subscription database). 2007. http://galenet.galegroup.com./ Last visited June 2009.

Hamilton-Selway, Joanne. "Bertrice Small." In *Romance Today: An A-To-Z Guide to Contemporary American Romance Writers.* Ed. John Charles and Shelley Mosley. Westport, CT: Greenwood. 2007. pp. 354–356.

Thurston, Carol. "Bertrice Small." In *Twentieth-Century Romance and Historical Writers.* Ed. Aruna Vasudevan. 3rd ed. London: St. James Press. 1990. pp. 608–609.

Biographies and Interviews

"ARR Interview with Bertrice Small." *A Romance Review.* March 2003. http://www.aromancereview.com/interviews/bertricesmall.phtml. Last visited September 2009.

"Bertrice Small." *Veronika Asks.* September 30, 2009. http://veronikaasks. wordpress.com/2009/09/30/bertrice-small. Last visited October 2009.

"Bertrice Small." *Rachelle Chase.* May 27, 2007. http://rachellechase.com/chatting-with-chase/bertrice-small/. Last visited September 2009.

"Bertice Small Interview." *Fallen Angel Reviews.* 2004. http://fallenangelreviews.com/Interviews/2004/Jul04-JoAnn-BertriceSmall.htm. Last visited September 2009.

"Bullough, Jenny. "Author Bertrice Small's Wild and Sexy Faeries." *Harlequin's Paranormal Romance Blog.* May 5, 2008. http://paranormalromanceblog.com/2008/05/05/author-bertrice-smalls-wild-and-sexy-faeries/. Last visited September 2009.

Falk, Kathryn. "Bertrice Small." *Love's Leading Ladies.* New York: Pinnacle Books. 1982. pp. 259–263.

Saville, Susanne. "Bertrice Small at The Chatty Cat Café." *Susan Saville's Caffeinated Natter.* December 3, 2008. http://myblog.susannesaville.com/2008/12/03/bertrice-small-at-the-chatty-cat-cafe.aspx. Last visited September 2009.

Web Sites

Bertrice Small. http://www.bertricesmall.net/. Last visited December 2009. Bertrice Small's official Web site; includes, a brief biography, a backlist of titles, a message board for her fans, photos, and an FAQ.

LaVyrle Spencer (1943–)

Contemporary / Historical / Category

Biographical Sketch

LaVyrle Spencer was so inspired by Kathleen Woodiwiss's novel *The Flame and the Flower* that she began writing herself. After finishing her first novel, *The Fulfillment,* Spencer mailed the manuscript to Woodiwiss. Woodiwiss was so moved by the story that she sent it on to her publishing house, and Spencer's writing career began. Since she was still working full-time as a teacher, Spencer had to arrange her writing schedule around her career and her family. In 1989, Spencer retired from writing to enjoy time with her family. Spencer is a member of the Romance Writers of America Hall of Fame.

Spencer's novels were a departure from the "bodice ripper" type novels that were the mainstay of romance publishing in the late 1970s and early 1980s because unlike many of those stories, the characters are what drive a Spencer novel. The characters are flawed human beings, trying to get through life the best way they can. Spencer's books exhibit some sensuality but the morality of the characters is always a main point.

Anna Reardon had done the unforgivable. She had lied through her teeth to get Karl Lindstrom to marry her! She had intentionally deceived the man in order to get him to send her passage money to Minnesota as his mail-order bride.

LaVyrle Spencer
The Endearment, 1982

Major Works

Novels

Then Came Heaven, 1997
Small Town Girl, 1997
That Camden Summer, 1996
Home Song, 1995
Family Blessings, 1994
November of the Heart, 1993
Bygones, 1992
Forgiving, 1991
Bittersweet, 1990
Morning Glory, 1989

Vows, 1988
Years, 1986
Separate Beds, 1985
Twice Loved, 1984
Sweet Memories, 1984
The Gamble, 1984
Hummingbird, 1983
The Endearment, 1982
The Fulfillment, 1979

Category Novels

The Hellion, Harlequin Super Romance #130, 1984
Spring Fancy, Harlequin Temptation #1, 1984
A Promise to Cherish, Second Chance at Love, #100, 1983
Forsaking All Others, Second Chance at Love, #76, 1982

Other Works

Movies Based on the Novels of LaVyrle Spencer

Foch, Nina and Raffin, Deborah, director. *Family Blessings,* CBS TV. February 2, 1999. Internet Movie Database, http://www.imdb.com/title/tt0136866./ Last visited September 2009.

Haggard, Piers, director. *The Fulfillment of Mary Gray,* CBS TV. February 19, 1989. Internet Movie Database, http://www.imdb.com/title/tt0097401/. Last visited September 2009.

Malone, Nancy, director. *Home Song,* CBS TV. March 20, 1996. Internet Movie Database, http://www.imdb.com/title/tt0116549/. Last visited September 2009.

Stern, Steven Hilliard, director. *Morning Glory.* 1993. Internet Movie Database, http://www.imdb.com/title/tt0107604/. Last visited September 2009.

Research Sources

Encyclopedias and Handbooks

"LaVyrle Spencer." *Literature Resource Center.* (subscription database). 2008. http://galenet.galegroup.com/. Last visited June 2009.

Thurston, Carol. "LaVyrle Spencer." In *Twentieth-Century Romance and Historical Writers.* Ed. Aruna Vasudevan. 3rd ed. London: St. James Press. 1990. pp. 615–616.

Biographies and Interviews

Falk, Kathryn. "LaVyrle Spencer." *Love's Leading Ladies.* New York: Pinnacle Books. 1982. pp. 265–268.

"LaVyrle in Bloom." *Mpls. St. Paul,* Volume 21, Issue 10, October 1993. p. 74.

"LaVyrle Spencer." *Good Housekeeping,* Volume 220, Issue 2, February 1995. p. 152.

Rozen, Leah. "Isn't It Romantic." *Woman's Day,* Volume 56, Issue 1, November 24, 1992. p. 44.

Criticism and Readers' Guides

Chappel, Deborah. "LaVyrle Spencer and the Anti-Essentialist Argument." *Paradoxa: Studies in World Literary Genres,* Volume 3, Issues 1–2, 1997. pp. 107–120.

Chappel, Deborah Kay. *American Romances: Narratives of Culture and Identity.* PhD Dissertation. Duke University. 1991.

Mary Stewart (1916–)

Romantic Suspense / Historical / Medieval / Paranormal

Biographical Sketch

English-born Mary Stewart attended the University of Durham, where she received a bachelor of arts degree and a master's degree. She later married Sir Frederick Henry Stewart.

Stewart is one of the founders of the romantic suspense genre in romance, and her first nine novels set the foundation for the genre. While the stories may not have the action of today's romantic suspense stories, the level of suspense keeps the stories interesting. Stewart then wrote a trilogy about Merlin, one of the most critically reviewed works by a romance and fantasy author. In later years, Stewart's stories included paranormal elements further pushing the romance genre. In 1992 Stewart received the Lifetime Achievement Award by the Romance Writers of America. She lives in Scotland.

> Moravik had the biggest collection of charms and talismans of anyone in Maridunim, and I had never known her pass a wayside shrine without paying respects to whatever image inhabited it, but officially she was a Christian and, when in trouble, a devout one.

Mary Stewart
The Chrystal Cave, 1970

Major Works

Novels in Series

Merlin Trilogy

The Last Enchantment, 1979
The Hollow Hills, 1973
The Crystal Cave, 1970

Novels

Rose Cottage, 1997	*Airs Above the Ground*, 1965
The Prince and the Pilgrim, 1995	*This Rough Magic*, 1964
The Stormy Petrel, 1991	*The Moon-Spinners*, 1962
Thornyhold, 1988	*The Ivy Tree*, 1961
The Wicked Day, 1983	*My Brother Michael*, 1959
A Walk in Wolf Wood, 1980	*Nine Coaches Waiting*, 1958
Touch Not the Cat, 1976	*Thunder on the Right*, 1957
Ludo and the Star Horse, 1975	*Wildfire at Midnight*, 1956
The Little Broomstick, 1972	*Madam, Will You Talk?* 1955
The Gabriel Hounds, 1967	

Research Sources

For additional resources about Mary Stewart, search the MLA Bibliography or consult with your librarian. Below is a sample of resources.

Encyclopedias and Handbooks

"Mary Stewart." *Literature Resource Center.* (subscription database). 2008. http://galenet.galegroup.com/. Last visited June 2009.

Mussell, Kay. "Mary Stewart." In *Twentieth-Century Romance and Historical Writers.* Ed. Aruna Vasudevan. 3rd ed. London: St. James Press, 1990. pp. 630–631.

Biographies and Interviews

Friedman, Lenemaja. *Mary Stewart.* Boston: Twayne Publishers. 1990.

Criticism and Readers' Guides

Fries, Maureen. "The Rationalization of the Arthurian 'Matter' in T. H. White and Mary Stewart." *Philological Quarterly,* Volume 56, 1977. pp. 258–265.

Herman, Harold J. "The Women in Mary Stewart's Merlin Trilogy." *Interpretations: A Journal of Idea, Analysis, and Criticism,* Volume 15, Issue 2, Spring 1984. pp. 101–114.

Jurich, Marilyn. "Mithraic Aspects of Merlin in Mary Stewart's *The Crystal Cave.*" In *The Celebration of the Fantastic: Selected Papers from the Tenth Anniversary International Conference on the Fantastic in the Arts.* Ed. Donald E. Morse, Csilla Bertha, and Marshall B. Tymn. Westport, CT: Greenwood Press. 1992. pp. 91–101.

Nelson, Marie. "King Arthur and the Massacre of the May Day Babies: A Story Told by Sir Thomas Malory, Later Retold by John Steinbeck, Mary Stewart, and T. H. White." *Journal of the Fantastic in the Arts,* Volume 11, Issue 3, 2000. pp. 266–281.

Watson, Jeanie. "Mary Stewart's Merlin: Word of Power." *Arthurian Interpretations,* Volume 1, Issue 2, Spring 1987. pp. 70–83.

Wiggins, Kayla McKinney. "I'll Never Laugh at a Thriller Again: Fate, Faith and Folklore in the Mystery Novels of Mary Stewart." *Clues: A Journal of Detection,* Volume 21, Issue 1, Spring–Summer 2000. pp. 49–60.

Web Site

Mary Stewart does not have an official Web site.

Anne Stuart (1948–)

Romantic Suspense / Contemporary / Historical / Medieval /Paranormal / Category

Biographical Sketch

Anne Stuart grew up in a dysfunctional family which she credits for her career as a writer; without her troubled background, Stuart may not have escaped into the Gothic novels of Victoria Holt and the Regency novels of Georgette Heyer. At the age of 25, Stuart wrote her first novel, and she's been writing every since. Stuart lives in Vermont with her husband, two children, and a very large yard.

Stuart's novels, historical or contemporary, are not light, happy romances. Her heroes are dark, elegant, ruthless, with very few redeeming qualities, and they follow their own moral code, which may be at odds with that of society. The heroines are equally tortured, and only the love between the two helps the characters to find peace. The stories take place in a variety of locations and time periods, allowing Stuart the opportunity to write for many different romance audiences. In 1996, Stuart received the Lifetime Achievement Award from the Romance Writers of America.

> *Reno bounded up the stairs, two at a time, and pushed open the door to the deserted apartment, only to stare directly into the barrel of a Glock.*
>
> Anne Stuart
> *Fire and Ice,* 2008

Major Works

Novels in Series

House of Rohan

Ruthless, 2010
Reckless, 2010
Breathless, 2010

Ice Series

Fire and Ice, 2008
Ice Storm, 2007
Ice Blue, 2007
Cold as Ice, 2006
Black Ice, 2005

Maggie Bennett

At the Edge of the Sun, 1987
Darkness Before the Dawn, 1987
Escape Out of Darkness, 1987

Novels

Silver Falls, 2009
The Devil's Waltz, 2006
Hidden Honor, 2004
Into the Fire, 2003
Still Lake, 2002
The Widow, 2001
Lady Fortune, 2000
Shadows at Sunset, 2000
Shadow Lover, 1999
Prince of Magic, 1998
Lord of Danger, 1997

Ritual Sins, 1997
Prince of Swords, 1996
Moonrise, 1996
Nightfall, 1995
To Love a Dark Lord, 1994
Shadow Dance, 1993
A Rose at Midnight, 1993
Seen and Not Heard, 1988
The Houseparty, 1985
Barrett's Hill, 1974

Category Novels

Harlequin Intrigue

Night and Day: Night, #637, 2001
The Fall of Maggie Brown, 2000
Winter's Edge, #329, 1995
Catspaw II, #103, 1988
Hand in Glove, #59, 1987
Catspaw, #9, 1985
Tangled Lies, #5, 1984

Harlequin American Romance

Burning Bright, #1041, 2004
Wild Thing, #845, 2000
The Right Man, #765, 1999
A Dark & Stormy Night, #702, 1997
The Soldier & the Baby, #573, 1995
Cinderman, #525, 1994
Falling Angel, #513, 1993
One More Valentine, #473, 1993
Rafe's Revenge, #453, 1992
Heat Lightning, #434, 1992
Chasing Trouble, #413, 1991
Night of the Phantom, #398, 1991
Lazarus Rising, #374, 1991
Angels Wings, #361, 1990
Rancho Diablo, #346, 1990
Crazy Like a Fox, #326, 1990
Glass Houses, #311, 1989
Cry for the Moon, #260, 1988
Partners in Crime, #246, 1988
Blue Sage, #213, 1987
Bewitching Hour, #177, 1986
Rocky Road, #126, 1985
Housebound, #93, 1985
Museum Piece, #52, 1984
Heart's Ease, #39, 1984
Chain of Love, #30, 1983

Candlelight Romance

The Spinster and the Rake, #711, 1982
Lord Satan's Bride, #649, 1981
The Demon Count's Daughter, #561, 1980
The Demon Count, #557, 1980
Demonwood, #523, 1979

Other Category Novels

Break the Night, Silhouette Shadows #9, 1993
Now You See Him, Silhouette Intimate Moments #429, 1992
Special Gifts, Silhouette Intimate Moments #321, 1990
Against the Wind, Candlelight Ecstasy Supreme #84, 1985
Banish Misfortune, Harlequin American Romance Premiere #5, 1985

Collaborations

With Jennifer Crusie and Lani Diane Rich

Dogs and Goddesses, 2009

With Eileen Dreyer and Jennifer Crusie

The Unfortunate Miss Fortunes, 2007

Research Sources

Encyclopedias and Handbooks

"Anne Stuart." *Literature Resource Center.* (subscription database). 2006. http://galenet.galegroup.com/. Last visited June 2009.

Biographies and Interviews

"Anne Today, Anne Tomorrow: A Q&A with Anne Stuart." *All About Romance.* March 3, 2000. http://www.likesbooks.com/annestuart.html. Last visited September 2009.

"At the Back Fence Issue #200." *All About Romance.* May 1, 2005. http://www.likesbooks.com/200.html#anne. Last visited September 2009.

Ward, Jean Marie. "Anne Stuart: Dark Romances." *Crescent Blues.* December 25, 2005. http://www.crescentblues.com/2_2issue/stuart.shtml. Last visited September 2009.

"Writer's Corner: Anne Stuart." *All About Romance.* October 2006. http://www.likesbooks.com/annestuart2006.html. Last visited September 2009.

Web Site

Anne Stuart. http://www.anne-stuart.com/. Last visited December 2009. The official Web site for Anne Stuart; includes biographical information, a backlist of titles, and a blog.

Susan Wiggs

Contemporary / Historical

Biographical Sketch

Susan Wiggs began writing as a child and after a detour as a teacher, returned to writing. Wiggs graduated from Stephen F. Austin State University and received a master's degree from Harvard University. In 1980 she married her husband Jay and became a math teacher. After finishing a romance novel and not having another to read, Wiggs began writing her own novel and published *Texas Wildflower* three years later, in 1987.

Wiggs writes emotional, character-driven stories that rarely follow the "girl meets boy" story line. Her characters, both heroes and heroines, are often recovering from divorce, a death, or some other adverse circumstance that can happen to real people and some of her stories are more women's fiction than romance. Wiggs's series feature a sense of place as well as the opportunity to revisit characters, and her settings and time periods are varied.

"I understand," she said at last. And she did, on one level. On another, she was devastated. Her heart was stunned. She couldn't quite feel it in her chest. Yet she knew when the numbness passed, she would feel it shatter.

Susan Wiggs
Fireside, 2009

Major Works

Novels in Series

The Lake Side Chronicles

Summer Hideaway, 2010
Lakeshore Christmas, 2009
Fireside, 2009
Snowfall at Willow Lake, 2008
Dockside, 2007
The Winter Lodge, 2007
Summer at Willow Lake, 2006

Calhoun Chronicles

A Summer Affair, 2003
Enchanted Afternoon, 2002
Halfway to Heaven, 2001
The Horsemaster's Daughter, 1999
The Charm School, 1999

Chicago Fire

The Firebrand, 2001
The Mistress, 2000
The Hostage, 2000

Tudor Rose Books

At the Queen's Summons (originally published as *Dancing on Air*), 1996
The Maiden's Hand (originally published as *Vows Made in Wine*), 1995
At the King's Command (originally published as *Circle in the Water*), 1994

Discovery Trilogy Books

Kingdom of Gold, 1994
Jewel of the Sea, 1993
October Wind, 1991

Novels

Just Breathe, 2008
Lakeside Cottage, 2005
Table for Five, 2005
Summer by the Sea, 2004
The Ocean Between Us, 2004
Home Before Dark, 2003
Passing Through Paradise, 2002
The You I Never Knew, 2001
The Drifter, 1998
The Lightkeeper, 1997

Miranda, 1996
Lord of the Night, 1993
The Mist and the Magic, 1993
The Raven and the Rose, 1991
The Lily and the Leopard, 1991
Moonshadow, 1989
Winds of Glory, 1988
Embrace the Day, 1988
Briar Rose, 1987
Texas Wildflower, 1987

Category Novels

Husband for Hire, Heart of the West #1, 1999

Other Works

"Write Byte: Feeding the Soul." *All About Romance*. October 23, 1997. http://www.likesbooks.com/wiggs.html. Last visited December 2009.

Research Sources

Encyclopedias and Handbooks

Mosley, Shelley. "Susan Wiggs". In *Romance Today: An A-To-Z Guide to Contemporary American Romance Writers*. Ed. John Charles and Shelley Mosley. Westport, CT: Greenwood. 2007. pp. 381–383.
"Susan Wiggs." *Literature Resource Center*. (subscription database). 2008. http://galenet.galegroup.com/. Last visited December 2009.

Biographies and Interviews

Bexte, Martina. "Susan Wiggs." *Bookloons*. September 2003. http://www.bookloons.com/cgi-bin/Columns.asp?type=Interview&name=Susan%20Wiggs. Last visited December 2009.
Fox, Suzanne. "PW Talks with Susan Wiggs." *Publisher's Weekly*, Volume 249, Issue 4, January 28, 2002. p. 277.
Housley, Suzie. "Her Pen is Mightier Than a Sword: An Interview with Susan Wiggs." *Beneath the Covers Past*. June 2002. http://www.myshelf.com/beneaththecovers/02/wiggs.htm. Last visited December 2009.
"LaFevers, R. L. "Meet Fellow Violet—Susan Wiggs." *Shrinking Violets*. January 29, 2009. http://shrinkingvioletpromotions.blogspot.com/2009/01/meet-fellow-violet-susan-wiggs.html. Last visited December 2009.

Rocks, Bonnie. "Writerspace Talks with Romance Author Susan Wiggs." *Writerspace.* http://www.writerspace.com/interviews/wiggs0202.html. Last visited December 2009.

"Susan Wiggs—And Now (As Usual), Something New." *All About Romance.* May 25, 2003. http://www.likesbooks.com/susanwiggs.html. Last visited December 2009.

Ward, Jean Marie and Smith, Teri. "Susan Wiggs: Historical Polish, Organizational Savvy." *Crescent Blues e-Magazine,* Volume 3, Issue 4. http://www.crescentblues.com/3_4issue/wiggs.shtml. Last visited December 2009.

Williams, Juan. "Interview: Two Romance Novelists Define and Defend the Genre." *Talk of the Nation.* National Public Radio. July 24, 2000.

Criticism and Readers' Guides

Therrien, Kathleen Mary. *Trembling at Her Own Response: Resistance and Reconciliation in Mass-Market Romance Novels.* PhD Dissertation, University of Delaware, 1997.

Web Site

Susan Wiggs. http://www.susanwiggs.com/free_books.shtml. Last visited December 2009. The offical Web site for Wiggs; includes a backlist of titles, guides for readers' groups, biographical information, a list of her upcoming appearances, and an FAQ.

Kathleen E. Woodiwiss (1939–2007)

Historical

Biographical Sketch

Kathleen Woodiwiss was born in Louisiana and married young. Her husband was in the Air Force and for the first part of her marriage they lived in Japan. After settling back in Kansas and then Minnesota, Woodiwiss began to write, mainly because she could not find anything good to read. After a divorce, she devoted time to raising her family and her writing.

Woodiwiss is credited with popularizing the historical romance genre. At the time that *The Flame and the Flower* was published only Gothic or romantic suspense novels were available. Woodiwiss used a historical setting, but added graphic sex scenes, a completely new innovation in a romance novel. Her heroines are strong and independent women doing what they can to survive, while the heroes follow the dominant, alpha male pattern of toughness. In 1988, Woodiwiss received the Lifetime Achievement Award by the Romance Writer's of America. Woodiwiss died of cancer in July of 2007.

The miserable night masked the passage of a carriage that careened through the narrow streets as if it fled from some terrible disaster. It jolted and tottered precariously over the cobblestones, its high wheels sending mud and water splattering.

Kathleen E. Woodiwiss
Shanna, 1977

Major Works

Novels

Everlasting, 2007
The Reluctant Suitor, 2003
A Season Beyond a Kiss, 2000
The Elusive Flame, 1998
Petals on the River, 1997
Forever in Your Embrace, 1992

So Worthy My Love, 1989
Come Love a Stranger, 1984
A Rose in Winter, 1982
Ashes in the Wind, 1979
Shanna, 1977
The Wolf and the Dove, 1974
The Flame and the Flower, 1972

Research Sources

Encyclopedias and Handbooks

"Kathleen E. Woodiwiss." *Literature Resource Center.* 2007. http://galenet.galegroup.com/. Last visited June 2009.
Radway, Janice. "Kathleen E. Woodiwiss." In Twentieth Century Romance and Historical Writers. Ed. Aruna Vasudevan. 3rd ed. London: St. James Press. 1990. pp. 729–730.

Biographies and Interviews

Breu, Giovanna. "Romance Writer Kathleen Woodiwiss is Passionate about Horse—and Happy Endings. *People.* February 7, 1983. p. 75.
Dukes, Jessica. "Meet the Writers: Kathleen E. Woodiwiss." *Barnes & Noble.* http://www.barnesandnoble.com/writers/writerdetails.asp?cid=1056927. Last visited September 2009.
Falk, Kathryn. "Kathleen Woodiwiss." *Love's Leading Ladies.* New York: Pinnacle Books. 1982. pp. 327–331.
Fox, Margalit. "Kathleen Woodiwiss: Novelist, Dies at 68." *New York Times.* July 12, 2007. p. B7.
Klemesrud, Judy. "Behind the Best Sellers." *New York Times Book Review,* Volume 84, November 4, 1979. p. 52.
"PW Interviews." *Publishers Weekly,* Volume 211, May 30, 1977. pp. 6–7.

Criticism and Readers' Guides

Hinnant, Charles H. "Desire and the Marketplace: A Reading of Kathleen Woodiwiss's *The Flame and the Flower*." In *Doubled Plots: Romance and History*. Ed. Susan Strehle and Mary Paniccia. Jackson, MS: Mississippi University Press. 2003. pp. 147–164.

Petersen, Clarence. "A Tender, Wicked, Sweet, Savage Saga of Money and Romance." *Chicago Tribune*. July 9, 1978. p. F1.

Web Site

Kathleen E. Woodiwiss. http://www.harpercollins.com/authors/15300/Kathleen_E_ Woodiwiss/index.aspx. Last visited December 2009. HarperCollins Publishers Web site for Woodiwiss; includes a brief biography and a book list.

Glossary of Romance Terms

Below is a select list of terms used in the discussion of romance novels. For a list of additional terms please visit the Windy City RWA chapter Web site, http://www.windycityrwa.org/pages/node/29 or Candice Hern's Regency Glossary, http://www.candicehern.com/bookshelf/glossary.htm.

Almack's An assembly room that held an exclusive subscription ball every Wednesday during the Season that is featured in many Regency novels.

Alpha Male An uber-dominant, stubborn, tough hero who usually exhibits cruel tendencies to the heroine. See Elizabeth Lowell's Silhouette Desire novels.

ARC Advanced Reading Copy, a pre-published proof of a novel.

Bodice Ripper The cover of a historical novel featuring the heroine bursting out of her dress. See any older edition of a Johanna Lindsey novel.

Rita Award Annual award given by the Romance Writers of America.

The Season The social season in Regency England; it begins in spring and runs through June.

Series Romance A category series romance novel, i.e., Silhouette Special Edition.

Ton The fashionable society or the aristocracy in Regency England.

Too-Stupid-To-Live-Heroine Usually young, very impetuous; always puts herself in a dangerous situation by not listening to the hero.

Wallbanger The book that is so bad that the reader wants to throw it across the room into the wall.

Bibliography and List of Research Sources

The following list of sources serves two purposes—first, to list all the print and most of the Internet sources used in the production of this book and second, to list additional titles to assist students and researchers with finding information on romance authors and the romance genre.

Encyclopedias and Handbooks

Charles, John and Mosley, Shelley, Eds. *Romance Today: An A to Z Guide to Contemporary American Romance Writers.* Westport, CT: Greenwood Publishers. 2007.

Contemporary Authors, 1981 to the present. Detroit, MI: Gale.

Dictionary of Literary Biography, 1978 to the present. Detroit, MI: Gale.

Both *Contemporary Authors* and *Dictionary of Literary Biography* are available online via the Literature Resource Center

Twentieth-Century Romance and Historical Writers. Ed. Vasudevan, Aruna. 3rd ed. London: St. James Press. 1990.

Books

Betz, Phyllis M. *Lesbian Romance Novels: A History and Critical Analysis.* Jefferson, NC: McFarland. 2009.

Falk, Kathryn. *Love's Leading Ladies.* New York: Pinnacle Books. 1982.

Frantz, Sarah S. G. and Rennhak, Katharina, Eds. *Women Constructing Men: Female Novelists and their Male Characters, 1750–2000.* Lanham, MD: Lexington Books. 2009.

Goade, Sally, Ed. *Empowerment Versus Oppression: Twenty-First Century Views of Popular Romance Novels.* Newcastle, UK: Cambridge Scholars Publishers. 2007.

Guiley, Rosemary. *Love Lines: A Romance Reader's Guide to Printed Pleasure.* New York: Facts on File Publications. 1983.

Jaegly, Peggy J. *Romantic Hearts: A Personal Reference for Romance Readers.* 3rd ed. Lanham, MD: Scarecrow Press. 1997.

Jensen, Margaret Ann. *Love's Sweet Return: The Harlequin Story.* Bowling Green, OH: Bowling Green State University Popular Press. 1984.

Krentz, Jayne Ann, Ed. *Dangerous Men & Adventurous Women: Romance Writers on the Appeal of the Romance.* Philadelphia, PA: University of Pennsylvania Press. 1992.

Modleski, Tania. *Loving with a Vengeance: Mass-Produced Fantasies for Women.* 2nd ed. New York: Routledge. 2008.

Mussell, Kay and Tunon, Johanna, Eds. *North American Romance Writers.* Lanham, MD: Scarecrow Press. 1999.

Radway, Janice. *Reading the Romance: Women, Patriarchy and Popular Literature.* Chapel Hill, NC: University of North Carolina Press. 1984.

Ramsdell, Kristin. *Romance Fiction: A Guide to the Genre.* Englewood, CO: Libraries Unlimited. 1999.

Ramsdell, Kristin. *What Romance Do I Read Next: A Reader's Guide to Recent Romance Fiction.* Detroit, MI: Gale Research. 1997.

Regis, Pamela. *A Natural History of the Romance Novel.* Philadelphia, PA: University of Pennsylvania Press. 2003.

Schurman, Lydia Cushman and Johnson, Deidre. *Scorned Literature: Essays on the History and Criticism of Popular Mass-Produced Fiction in America.* Westport, CT: Greenwood Press. 2002.

Uszkurat, Carol Ann. "Mid Twentieth Century Lesbian Romance: Reception and Redress." *Outwrite: Lesbianism and Popular Culture.* Ed. Gabriele Griffin. London: Pluto Press. 1993. pp. 26–47.

Wendell, Sarah and Tan, Candy. *Beyond Heaving Bosoms: The Smart Bitches Guide to Romance Novels.* New York: Simon and Schuster. 2009.

Magazines and Academic Journals

Affaire de Coeur Magazine, 1979 to the present. Book reviews and articles on writing romance novels.

Clark, Beverly Lyon, Karen, Bernier, Gennari, Henneberry-Nassau, Michelle, Jenks, Lauren Beth, Moorman, Angie J., and Rhodes, Marah Bianca. "Reading Romance, Reading Ourselves." *The Centennial Review,* Volume 40, Issue 2, 1996. pp. 359–384.

Journal of Popular Romance Studies, 2010 to the present. http://jprstudies.org/issues/issue-1-1/. Scholarly articles on the romance genre.

Para-Doxa: Studies in World Literary Genres, published by Delta Publications, *http://paradoxa.com/.* Volume 3, Issue 1–2, 1997, was devoted to scholarly research of the romance genre and romance authors.

Romantic Times Book Reviews, 1981 to the present. Unfortunately this title is not indexed in major databases and very few libraries have the entire publication run.

Selinger, Eric Murphy. "Rereading the Romance." *Contemporary Literature,* Volume 48, Issue 2, 2007. pp. 307–324.

Research Databases

The following resources are research databases found in most academic or large public library systems. Please check with your library regarding access to these resources.

Academic Search Complete from EbscoHost
ProQuest Research Library from ProQuest.
Multidisciplinary databases that contain newspaper, magazine, and scholarly articles about romance authors and the romance genre. These also serve as strong resources for book reviews of romance novels. These databases are only available by subscription, so please visit your local library for information.

Dissertation Abstracts or *Digital Dissertations* from ProQuest.
Resources provide full-text access to PhD dissertations and master's theses from 1997 to the present and indexes PhD dissertations from 1861. This database is only available by subscription so please contact your local library for more information.

Literature Online database from Chadwyck-Healey. Provides access to classic works of literature and literary criticism found in journal articles. Reference sources are also indexed. This database is only available by subscription, so please visit your local library for more information.

Literature Resource Center from Gale Cengage Learning. This resource contains online versions of *Contemporary Authors* and other literature resources produced by Gale. This resource may also be updated more often than the print versions. This database is only available by subscription so please visit your local library for more information.

MLA International Bibliography from Gale Cengage Learning. Resource covers literary scholarship from 1926 to the present. Journal articles, book chapters, and other materials are indexed. This database is only available by subscription so please visit your local library for more information.

Online Resources

The following list of Web sites is a wonderful starting place for the romance reader to learn more about an author and for the romance scholar to begin the research process. Most of these Web sites were used in the production of this book.

All About Romance. http://www.likesbooks.com/home.html. This is possibly the best Web site for information about romance books and romance authors. Many authors contribute to the site through comments or writing a columns. This site is also a wonderful resource for reviews of romance novels.

Cherry Forums. http://www.cherryforums.com/index.php. A forum community for lovers of romance novels and Jennifer Crusie in particular. The forums are focused on book discussion, help with writing, and other topics, and allow anyone to participate.

Fiction DB. http://www.fictiondb.com/default.htm. This is a wonderful site that lists the complete works of an author. The author's book lists can be sorted alphabetically or by publication date. *This is one of the only online sources available for information about a specific novel in a category series, i.e., Silhouette Intimate Moments, #1000.*

Goddess Blogs. http://thegoddessblogs.com/. This site includes a group blog of several romance authors, including Rachel Gibson and Suzanne Enoch. Topics covered include writing, interviews, and everyday life topics.

A Romance Review. http://www.aromancereview.com/news/. A detailed Web site containing reviews of romance novels, interviews with authors, and columns about the romance genre. Some articles are dated.

Romance Wiki. http://www.romancewiki.com/Main_Page. The Romance Wiki is a Wikipedia style resource for authors, readers, and scholars of the romance genre. Author profiles, a list of romance books by title, and a bibliography are a few of the resources available.

Romancing the Blog. http://www.romancingtheblog.com/blog/. Multiauthor blog about the romance genre. The blog contains criticism and history of the romance genre.

The Romantic Bookcomer Website. http://www.die-buecherecke.de/e_index. htm. This site is authored by a German romance reader and features interviews with many popular romance authors. This blog provides a wonderful perspective on the romance genre from a non-U.S. perspective.

Running with Quills blog. http://www.runningwithquills.com/. This site includes the blogs of several romance authors including Jayne Ann Krentz and Elizabeth Lowell. Topics include a given author's writing process, the history of the romance genre, and general life events.

Smart Bitches, Trashy Books blog. http://www.smartbitchestrashybooks.com./ Possibly the most entertaining blog on romance ever created. Often snarky, occasionally mean, the authors never pull punches. The site contains book reviews and hard-hitting criticism of the romance genre.

Teach Me Tonight blog. http://teachmetonight.blogspot.com/. This is one of the first scholarly attempts to apply literary criticism to the romance genre. The blog is written by academics who are actively writing about the romance genre.

Word Wenches blog. http://wordwenches.typepad.com/word_wenches/. This is a combined blog of several historical romance authors including Mary Jo Putney, Jo Beverley, and formerly Loretta Chase. Topics include insightful interviews, history lessons, and the writing process.

Associations Web Sites

International Association for the Study of Popular Romance. http://iaspr.org/. According to the mission statement, the association is the first scholarly attempt to bring scholarly researchers of romance novels together. IASPR produces a refereed journal and an annual conference.

Romance Writers of America. http://www.rwanational.org/. The national organization to support romance writers. RWA awards the prestigious RITAs and holds a national conference.

Major Awards in Romance Fiction Won by Profiled Authors

Golden Heart Award

http://www.rwanational.org/cs/contests_and_awards/golden_heart_awards. Awarded by the Romance Writers of America to recognize outstanding manuscripts.

The Rita

http://www.rwanational.org/cs/contests_and_awards/rita_awards. Awarded by the Romance Writers of America for published romance fiction novels. Originally called the Golden Medallion Winner, the award was renamed "the Rita" in 1990.

Rita Winners Profiled in this Book

Jo Beverley

Devilish, Best Long Historical Romance, 2001
My Lady Notorious, Best Historical Series, 1994
Deidre and Don Juan, Best Regency Romance, 1994
An Unwilling Bride, Best Regency Romance, 1993
Emily and the Dark Angel, Best Regency Romance, 1992

Loretta Chase

Lord of Scoundrels, Best Short Historical, 1996
The Sandalwood Princess, Best Regency Romance, 1991

Jennifer Crusie

  Bet Me, Best Contemporary Single Title, 2005
  Getting Rid of Bradley, Best Short Contemporary Series Romance, 1995

Eileen Dreyer

  A Man to Die For, Best Single Title Contemporary, 1992

Kathleen Eagle

  This Time Forever, Best Single Title Contemporary, 1993

Rachel Gibson,

  Not Another Bad Date, Best Contemporary Single Title Romance, 2009
  True Confessions, Best Contemporary Single Title, 2002

Robin Lee Hatcher

  The Shepherd's Voice, Best Inspirational Romance, 2001
  Patterns of Love, Best Inspirational Romance, 1999

Judith Ivory

  The Proposition, Best Short Historical, 2000

Lisa Kleypas

  Worth Any Price, Best Short Historical, 2004
  "I Will" from Wish List, Best Romantic Novella, 2002

Kathleen Korbel

  A Soldier's Heart, Best Long Contemporary Series Romance, 1995
  A Rose for Maggie, Best Long Contemporary Series Romance , 1992
  The Ice Cream Man, Best Long Contemporary Series Romance, 1990
  Perchance to Dream, Best Romantic Suspense, 1990

Stephanie Laurens

  "The Fall of Rogue Gerard" in *It Happened One Night,* Best Romance
    Novella, 2009

Elizabeth Lowell

Untamed, Best Historical Single Title, 1994

Debbie Macomber

The Christmas Basket, Best Traditional Romance, 2003

Kasey Michaels

The Lurid Lady Lockport, Best Regency Romance, 1985

Julia Quinn

The Secret Diaries of Miss Miranda Cheever, Best Regency Historical Romance, 2008
On the Way To the Wedding, Best Long Historical Romance, 2007

Susan Elizabeth Phillips

First Lady, Best Contemporary Single, 2001
Dream A Little Dream, Best Contemporary Single Title, 1999
Nobody's Baby But Mine, RWA's Favorite Book of 1997
It Had To Be You, Best Romance of 1994

Mary Jo Putney

Dancing on the Wind, Best Long Historical Romance, 1995
The Rake and the Reformer, Best Regency Romance, 1990

Nora Roberts

Tribute, Best Novel with Strong Romantic Elements, 2009
Birthright, Best Contemporary Single Title, 2004
Remember When—Part 1, Best Romantic Suspense, 2004
Three Fates, Best Romantic Suspense, 2003
Carolina Moon, Best Romantic Suspense, 2001
Born in Ice, Best Romance of 1995, Contemporary Single Title, 1996
Hidden Riches, Best Romantic Suspense, 1995
Private Scandals, Best Contemporary Single Title, 1994
Nightshade, Best Romantic Suspense, 1994
Divine Evil, Best Romantic Suspense, 1993
Brazen Virtue, Best Suspense, 1989

One Summer, Best Long Contemporary Series Romance, 1987
A Matter of Choice, Best Long Contemporary Series Romance, 1985
Opposites Attract, Best Short Contemporary Romance, 1985
This Magic Moment, Best Contemporary 65-80,000 words, 1984
Untamed, Best Traditional Romance, 1984
The Heart's Victory, Best Contemporary Sensual Romance, 1983

J. D. Robb

Survivor in Death, Best Romantic Suspense, 2006

LaVyrle Spencer

Morning Glory, Best Romance of 1989
The Gamble, Best Historical Romance, 1988
Twice Loved, Best Historical Romance, 1985
Hummingbird, Best Historical Romance, 1984
The Endearment, Best Mainstream Historical Romance, 1983

Anne Stuart

Ice Blue, Best Romantic Suspense, 2008
Winter's Edge, Best Romantic Suspense, 1996
Falling Angel, Best Futuristic/Fantasy/Paranormal Romance, 1994
Banish Misfortune, Best Single Title Romance, 1986

Susan Wiggs

Lakeside Cottage, Best Contemporary Single Title, 2006
The Mistress, Best Short Historical, 2001
Lord of the Night, Best Romance of 1993

Romantic Times Magazine Career Achievement Award

http://www.rtbookreviews.com/rt-awards/nominees-and-winners?award_
type=author. Awarded by *Romantic Times Magazine* in many of the subgenres of romance. Selected winners include:

Mary Balogh

Simply Love, Historical Romance of the Year, 2006
Slightly Scandalous, Best Regency-Set Historical Romance, 2003

Terri Blackstock

Career Achievement Award, Inspirational, 2009

Loretta Chase

Don't Tempt Me, Historical Love & Laughter, 2009
Miss Wonderful, Best First Historical Romance, 2004

Jennifer Crusie

Contemporary Romance, 2009

Eileen Dreyer

Head Games, Best Suspense, 2005
Some Men's Dreams, Best Silhouette Intimate Moments, 2003

Christine Feehan

Mind Game, Best Historical Paranormal Fantasy, 2002

Heather Graham

Romantic Suspense/Intrigue, 2008

Candice Hern

In the Thrill of the Night, Regency-Set Historical Romance, 2006

Lisa Kleypas

Mine Till Midnight, Historical Romance of the Year, 2007

Jayne Ann Krentz

Falling Awake, Best Romantic Intrigue, 2004

Teresa Medeiros

Some Like it Wild, British Isle-Set Historical Romance, 2009
One Night of Scandal, Historical Romance, 2003

Kasey Michaels

Bowled Over, Amateur Sleuth, 2007

Cathie Linz

Series Storyteller of the Year, 1991–1992

Julia Quinn

It's in His Kiss, British Isle-Set Historical Romance, 2005

Mary Jo Putney

Loving a Lost Lord, Historical Knight in Shining Silver Hero Award, 2009

A Kiss of Fate, Best Historical Paranormal Fantasy, 2004

Christina Skye

To Catch a Thief, Romantic Intrigue, 2008

Bertrice Small

The Twilight Lord, Historical Paranormal, 2007

Anne Stuart

Fire and Ice, Romantic Suspense, 2008

RWA Nora Roberts Lifetime Achievement Award

http://www.rwanational.org/cs/contests_and_awards/lifetime_achievement. Awarded by the Romance Writers of America to recognize significant contributions to the romance genre. Winners include:

Debbie Macomber, 2010
Linda Lael Miller, 2007
Susan Elizabeth Phillips, 2006
Linda Howard, 2005
Heather Graham, 2003
Robin Lee Hatcher, 2001
Sandra Brown, 1998
Nora Roberts, 1997
Anne Stuart, 1996
Jayne Ann Krentz, 1995
Elizabeth Lowell, 1994
Kathleen Woodiwiss, 1988

Index

About the Author

SARAH E. SHEEHAN is the liaison librarian for the College of the Health & Human Services at George Mason University in Fairfax, VA.